SEW DOLLED UP

Creative Publishing international

© 2013 Boutique Sha, Inc.
Lady Boutique Series No. 3578 Felt no Kisekae Mascot

Originally published in Japanese language by Boutique Sha, Tokyo, Japan
English language rights, translation & production by World Book Media LLC
Email: info@worldbookmedia.com

Translators: Namiji Hatsuse and Kyoko Matthews
English edition editors: Lindsay Fair and Cassie Armstrong

First published in the United States of America by
Creative Publishing international, Inc., a member of
Quarto Publishing Group USA Inc.
400 First Avenue North
Suite 400
Minneapolis, MN 55401
1-800-328-3895
www.creativepub.com
Visit www.Craftside.Typepad.com for a behind-the-scenes peek at our crafty world!

ISBN: 978-1-58923-872-5

10 9 8 7 6 5 4 3 2 1

Library of Congress Cataloging-in-Publication Data not available at time of printing.

Printed in China

SEW DOLLED UP

Make Felt Dolls and Their Fun, Fashionable Wardrobes
with Fabric Scraps and Easy Hand Sewing

Boutique Sha

Creative Publishing
international

Table of Contents

Collection 1:
Country Style

Collection 2:
Uptown Girls

Collection 1:
Country Style

Meet our sweet and well-dressed dolls Irina and Anya.
They are country girls at heart and are inspired by
colorful and playful clothes.

These numbe[r]
indicate the diff[erent]
garments

4 + 9

2 + 8 + 18

Meet the Dolls

Use buttons to make arms that can move and wave!

Use yarn to make fun hairstyles!

Irina's light brown boots are easy to coordinate with many outfits.

Anya's favorite shoes are black Mary Janes.

Irina
Favorite Color: Blue
Prized Possession: Boo (her teddy bear)
Trademark: Long braids

Instructions on page 16

This collection is designed and handmade by Kuniko Kitamuki.

Back View

Anya
Favorite Color: Pink
Favorite Accessory: Pink headband
Trademark: Pigtail buns

Instructions on page 16

Outfit Ideas

Such a cute wardrobe and so many ways to mix and match!
Here are fun outfit ideas for dressing Irina and Anya.

3 + 11 + 14

Irina is wearing this
cheerful mix of the
Sleeveless Shirt (3)
and the Gingham
Pants (11) for a
Sunday picnic—
don't forget
the Flower
Tote (14)!

6

This Party Dress
(6) is great for
many celebrations.

1 + 7

Try this fun vintage red outfit
by coordinating the Tank Top
Blouse (1) and the Tiered Skirt (7).

5 + 10 + 15

Go for a Bohemian style by combining
the Vintage Vest (5), Linen Slacks (10),
and the Lace Purse (15).

4 + 5 + 10 + 17

Anya is going for a walk with her pooch. She's put together a perfect outfit for the occasion: Linen Slacks (10), Peter Pan Collar Blouse (4), and the fabulous Vintage Vest (5). Tie her hair up with the Lace Headband (17).

For more about the clothes and accessories
shown on the left and above, see pages 14-15.

The clothes in this collection fit both Irina and Anya. They like to share clothes and inspire each other with their different outfits.

3 + 7 + 17 + 19
Transform the green Sleeveless Shirt (3) by adding the Detachable Collar (19). Tie the outfit together with the polka dot and check Tiered Skirt (7) and the Lace Headband (17).

4 + 11 + 21
For a sweet and simple style, try the white Peter Pan Collar Blouse (4) with the Gingham Pants (11). Add a colorful accent with the Candy Necklace (21) made from beads.

Lace can be both casual and fancy. This pretty
detail makes any outfit more ladylike.

2 + 12 + 18 + 22

Dress for a playdate in the great outdoors
by sporting Blue Jeans (12), the Short Sleeve
Top (2), the pink Tie Headband (18), and of
course, Boo the Bear (22)!

6 + 15 + 20

For a special occasion put on the
Party Dress (6) and add a few dressy
accessories like the Flower Scarf
(20) and Lace Purse (15).

For more about the clothes and accessories
shown on the left and above, see pages 14–15.

2 + 9 + 13

For a colorful outfit, combine the Jumper Skirt (9), Short Sleeve Top (2), and Matryoshka Bag (13).

4 + 8 + 17

A sweet and neat everyday look: Peter Pa[n] Collar Blouse (4), Flora[l] Gathered Skirt (8), and Lace Headband (17).

3 + 5 + 7

Anya's going to a square dance! Coordinate the Vintage Vest (5) with the Tiered Skirt (7) and the Sleeveless Shirt (3) for a fun and stylish outfit.

1 + 10 + 16 + 20

How about a red and white outfit? Try the Crochet Cap (16), the Flower Scarf (20), and the Tank Top Blouse (1) with the Linen Slacks (10).

For more about the clothes and accessories shown on the left and below, see pages 14-15.

Look Boo, a storybook!

What's that creature?

Irina and Anya's Wardrobe

Tops and Dresses

Back View

Fastens in the back

1
Tank Top Blouse
Instructions on page 20

2
Short Sleeve Top
Instructions on page 20

3
Sleeveless Shirt
Instructions on page 21

4
Peter Pan Collar Blouse
Instructions on page 22

5
Vintage Vest
Instructions on page 23

6
Party Dress
Instructions on page 23

Skirts and Pants

7
Tiered Skirt
Instructions on page 25

8
Floral Gathered Skirt
Instructions on page 26

9
Jumper Skirt
Instructions on page 27

10

Linen Slacks
Instructions on page 28

11

Gingham Pants
Instructions on page 28

12

Blue Jeans
Instructions on page 29

Back View

The jeans even
have pockets!

Bags

13

Matryoshka Bag
Instructions on page 30

14

Flower Tote
Instructions on page 29

15

Lace Purse
Instructions on page 30

Accessories

16

Crochet Cap
Instructions on page 30

17

Lace Headband
Instructions on page 31

18

Tie Headband
Instructions on page 31

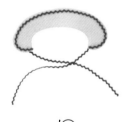

19

Detachable Collar
Instructions on page 31

20

Flower Scarf
Instructions on page 31

21

Candy Necklace
Instructions on page 28

22

Boo the Bear
Instructions on page 31

Irina and Anya
Shown on page 6

Materials (makes 1 doll)

Felt

- Cream: 6" x 8" (15 x 20 cm)
- Light blue (for Irina) or light pink (for Anya): 6" x 6" (15 x 15 cm)
- Light brown (for Irina) or maroon (for Anya): 4" x 6" (10 x 15 cm)
- Dark brown (for Irina) or yellow (for Anya): 2½" x 3⅛" (6 x 8 cm)
- Black (for Anya only): 2" x 4" (5 x 10 cm)
- Red: A small scrap

Notions

- #25 embroidery floss in same colors as felt (use 1 strand)
- Brown yarn in fingering-weight (for Irina)
- Yellow yarn in medium-weight (for Anya)
- Two ⅜" (1 cm) diameter white flower-shaped buttons
- Three ⅛" (0.3 cm) diameter buttons in different colors
- 15¾" (40 cm) of ¼" (0.7 cm) wide white picot ribbon
- Stuffing

Cutting Instructions

Trace and cut out the full-size templates on page 91. Pin or tape the templates to the felt and cut out following the instructions listed on the templates.

1. Make the body

a. Align the front hair and camisole with the body and attach using slip stitch. Follow the same process for the back. Sew the three ⅛" (0.3 cm) diameter buttons to the camisole on the front.

b. Embroider the eyes, nose, and mouth following the instructions on the body template. Glue the cheeks to the face.

c. Flip to the wrong side and trim each body a bit.

d. Align the front and back, then sew together using slip stitch. Leave an opening at the bottom and insert the stuffing.

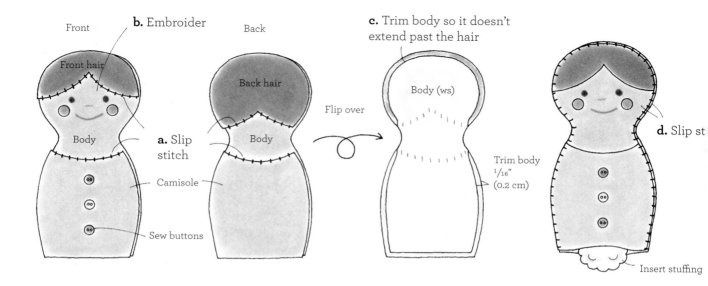

Front — Front hair — **b.** Embroider — Body — **a.** Slip stitch — Camisole — Sew buttons

Back — Back hair — Body — Flip over

c. Trim body so it doesn't extend past the hair — Body (ws) — Trim body 1/16" (0.2 cm)

d. Slip st — Insert stuffing

Make the legs

Irina

Align the pants with the legs and attach using slip stitch. Make two of each leg.

Embroider with running stitch.

Flip to the wrong side and trim each leg a bit.

Align the front and back for each leg, then sew together using blanket stitch. Insert the stuffing, leaving a bit of room at the top.

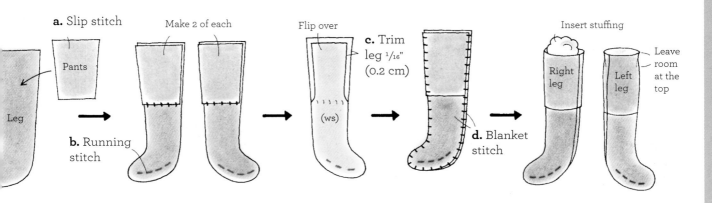

a. Slip stitch

Make 2 of each

Pants

Leg

b. Running stitch

Flip over

c. Trim leg ¹/₁₆" (0.2 cm)

(ws)

d. Blanket stitch

Insert stuffing

Right leg

Left leg

Leave room at the top

Anya

Align the pants and shoes with the legs and attach using slip stitch. Make two of each leg.

Align the front and back for each leg, then sew together using blanket stitch.

Insert the stuffing, leaving a bit of room at the top. Glue the straps to the shoes.

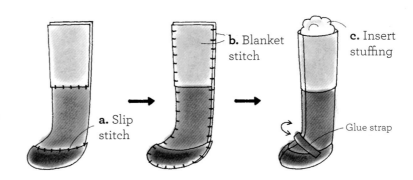

a. Slip stitch

b. Blanket stitch

c. Insert stuffing

Glue strap

Make the arms

Align two arms and sew together using blanket stitch, inserting the stuffing as you work. Repeat for the other arm.

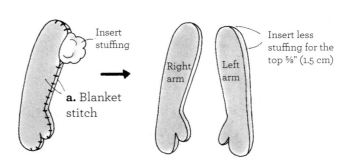

Insert stuffing

a. Blanket stitch

Right arm

Left arm

Insert less stuffing for the top ⅝" (1.5 cm)

4. Attach the arms and legs to the body

a. Insert the legs into the bottom opening of the body. Slip stitch the opening closed.

b. Glue a piece of ribbon around the neck.

c. Make a knot and stitch into the side seam at the position to attach the arm. Insert the needle through the arm, then through the button, before stitching back through the arm and the side seam. Knot the thread to secure. Repeat for the other arm.

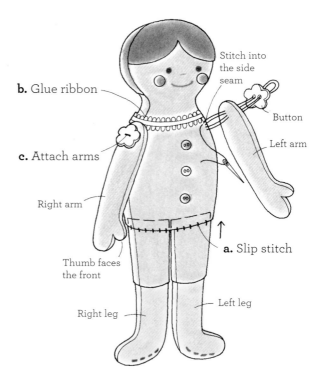

b. Glue ribbon

Stitch into the side seam

Button

Left arm

c. Attach arms

a. Slip stitch

Right arm

Thumb faces the front

Left leg

Right leg

5. Make the hair
For Irina

a. Align four 11¾" (30 cm) long strands of dark brown yarn and fold in half. Tie the yarn together at the fold using a sma scrap of yarn.

b. Separate the yarn into two groups of 3 strands and one group of 2 strands. Braid, then secure with a small scrap of yar

c. Repeat steps **a** and **b** to make another braid. Sew the braids to the back hair.

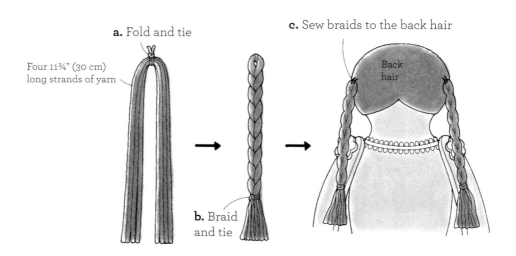

a. Fold and tie

c. Sew braids to the back hair

Four 11¾" (30 cm) long strands of yarn

Back hair

b. Braid and tie

or Anya

. Wrap the yellow yarn around a 1½" (4 cm) wide piece of cardboard 20 times.

. Remove the cardboard. Tightly tie the yarn together at the center using a small scrap of yarn.

. Repeat steps **a** and **b** to make another bun. Sew the buns to the back hair.

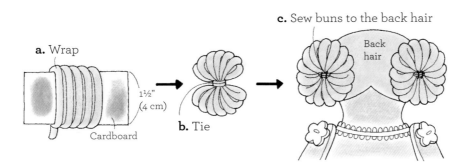

a. Wrap

1½"
(4 cm)

Cardboard

b. Tie

c. Sew buns to the back hair

Back hair

. **Finish the dolls**

. Glue pieces of ribbon around the camisole hem and the pants hem.

Irina

Anya

a. Glue ribbon

6¾" (17 cm) tall

1 Tank Top Blouse Shown on page 8

Materials

- Red felt: 4" x 8" (10 x 20 cm)
- #25 embroidery floss in red and white (use 1 strand)
- 7" (18 cm) of ¼" (0.5 cm) wide mint rickrack, 7" (18 cm) of ⅛" (0.3 cm) wide white rickrack, and 8" (20 cm) of ⅜" (1 cm) wide beige rickrack
- Two sets of ¼" (0.5 cm) diameter snaps

Full-size templates included on page 93.

1. Glue rickrack to the hem of each piece. Running stitch around the neck and arms. Zigzag stitch the beige rickrack.

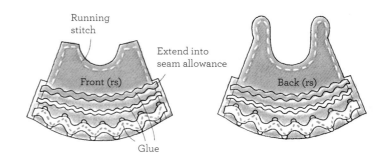

2. Align front and back pieces with right sides together. Sew along the sides.

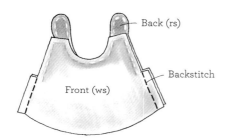

3. Turn right side out. Sew the snaps to each piece.

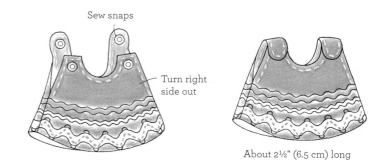

About 2½" (6.5 cm) long

2 Short Sleeve Top Shown on page 6

Materials

- Pink felt: 2½" x 2¾" (6 x 7 cm)
- Polka dot cotton fabric: 6" x 7" (15 x 18 cm)
- 6" (15 cm) of ¼" (0.6 cm) wide white lace
- #25 embroidery floss in pink (use 1 strand)
- Two sets of ¼" (0.5 cm) diameter snaps

Full-size templates included on page 96.

Tip: If the cotton fabric is too thin, adhere fusible interfacing to the wrong side.

1. Align the front and back pieces with right sides together. Sew along the shoulders and sides. Turn right side out.

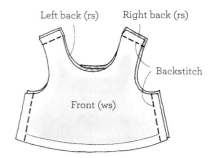

Fold the seam allowance along the center back and bottom. Hem using running stitch.

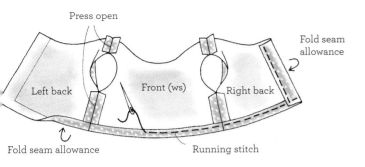

Press open

Left back

Front (ws)

Right back

Fold seam allowance

Fold seam allowance

Running stitch

3. Turn right side out. Align **a** on each sleeve and armhole, then slip stitch.

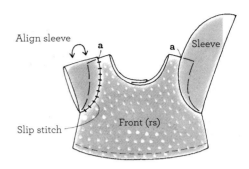

Align sleeve

a

a

Sleeve

Slip stitch

Front (rs)

Glue the lace to the neckline. Sew the snaps to the back pieces.

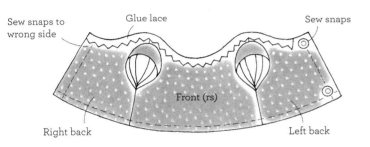

Sew snaps to wrong side

Glue lace

Sew snaps

Front (rs)

Right back

Left back

About 2½" (6.5 cm) long

3 Sleeveless Shirt Shown on page 8

Materials
- Light green felt: 4" x 8" (10 x 20 cm)
- #25 embroidery floss in light green and red (use 1 strand)
- 9¾" (25 cm) of ⅛" (0.3 cm) wide red rickrack
- Two sets of ¼" (0.5 cm) diameter snaps

Full-size templates included on page 93.

1. Glue rickrack to the hem of each piece.

Front

Glue rickrack

Left back

Right back

2. Align front and back pieces with right sides together. Sew along the shoulders and sides.

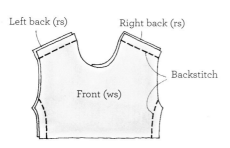

Left back (rs)   Right back (rs)

Backstitch

Front (ws)

3. Turn right side out. Sew the snaps to the back pieces. Running stitch around the neck.

Front

Running stitch

Left back

Right back

Turn right side out

Sew snaps

About 2½" (6 cm) long

4 Peter Pan Collar Blouse   Shown on page 6

Materials

- White felt: 4" x 8" (10 x 20 cm)
- #25 embroidery floss in white (use 1 strand)
- 9¾" (25 cm) of ⅛" (0.3 cm) wide white rickrack and 4" (10 cm) of ⅛" (0.3 cm) wide beige rickrack
- Two sets of ¼" (0.5 cm) diameter snaps

Full-size templates included on page 93.

1. Glue rickrack to the collar.

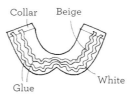

Collar   Beige

Glue   White

2. Glue collar to the front. Glue white rickrack to the hem of the front and both back pieces.

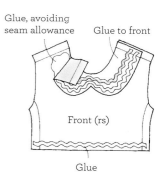

Glue, avoiding seam allowance   Glue to front

Front (rs)

Glue

3. Align front and back pieces with right sides together. Sew along the shoulders and sides.

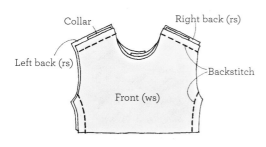

Collar   Right back (rs)

Left back (rs)

Backstitch

Front (ws)

4. Turn right side out. Sew the snaps to the back pieces.

Front

Left back

Right back

Turn right side out

Sew snaps

About 2½" (6 cm) long

Vintage Vest Shown on page 8

Materials

Black felt: 4" x 8" (10 x 20 cm)

Red felt: 1¼" x 2½" (3 x 6 cm)

Yellow, light green, and green felt: ¾" x 1¼" (2 x 3 cm) each

#25 embroidery floss in black, red, and white (use 1 strand)

11¾" (30 cm) of ⅛" (0.3 cm) wide red rickrack

Full-size templates included on page 92.

1. Glue rickrack to each front. Appliqué the flower and leaves to each front.

2. Align the front and back pieces with right sides together. Sew along the shoulders and sides. Turn right side out.

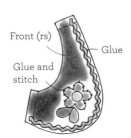
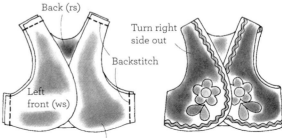

Party Dress Shown on page 8

Materials

Yellow felt: 3⅛" x 8" (8 x 20 cm)

Floral print cotton fabric: 3⅛" x 14½" (8 x 37 cm)

#25 embroidery floss in yellow (use 1 strand for the bodice)

Sewing thread to match the skirt fabric

6" (15 cm) of ⅛" (0.3 cm) wide white rickrack

6" (15 cm) of ¼" (0.6 cm) wide white lace

• Two sets of ¼" (0.5 cm) diameter snaps
• Three ¼" (0.4 cm) diameter pearl beads

A full-size template for the bodice is included on page 96. There is no template for the skirt. Refer to the step 3 diagram on page 24 for cutting dimensions. Seam allowance is included in the skirt cutting dimensions.

1. Align front and back bodice pieces with right sides together. Sew along the shoulders and sides.

2. Turn right side out. Sew the snaps to the back pieces.

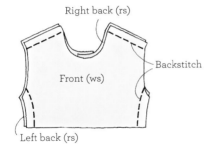
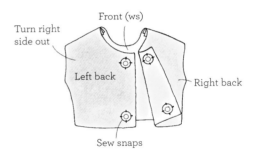

3. Fold the skirt hem over twice and blind stitch. Fold the skirt in half with right sides together and running stitch.

4. Loosely running stitch around the waist and pull the thread tails to gather.

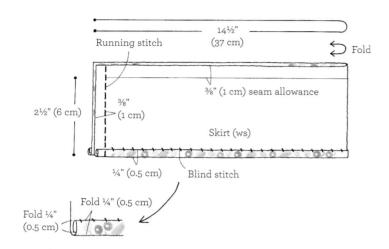

Running stitch

14½"
(37 cm)

⟲ Fold

⅜" (1 cm) seam allowance

⅜"
(1 cm)

2½" (6 cm)

Skirt (ws)

¼" (0.5 cm)

Blind stitch

Fold ¼" (0.5 cm)

Fold ¼"
(0.5 cm)

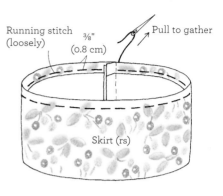

Running stitch
(loosely)

⅜"
(0.8 cm)

Pull to gather

Skirt (rs)

5. Glue the lace to the neckline. Adjust skirt gathers to make the waist the same size as the bodice, then knot the thread.

6. Tuck the skirt into the bodice and blind stitch.

7. Sew the pearl beads to the front and glue the rickrack to the wais[t]

Glue lace

Right
back

4 ¾"
(12 cm)

Knot

Skirt (rs)

Blind stitch

Front

⅜" (1 cm)

Tuck skirt
into bodice

Skirt (rs)

Glue
rickrack

About 5" (12.5 cm) long

Tiered Skirt Shown on page 8

Materials
Red gingham cotton fabric:
2" x 11" (5 x 28 cm)

Red polka dot cotton fabric:
2" x 19¾" (5 x 50 cm)

Sewing thread to match the fabric

31½" (80 cm) of ⅜" (0.8 cm) wide white lace

6" (15 cm) of ¼" (0.5 cm) wide elastic

There is no template for this project. Refer to the step 1 diagram for cutting dimensions. Seam allowance is included in the skirt cutting dimensions.

1. Cut the top and bottom sections of the skirt.

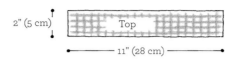

2" (5 cm)   Top   11" (28 cm)

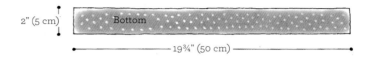

2" (5 cm)   Bottom   19¾" (50 cm)

Running stitch along the upper edge of the bottom section. Pull the thread tails to gather.

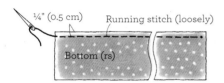

¼" (0.5 cm)   Running stitch (loosely)
Bottom (rs)

3. Gather until the bottom section is the same length as the top section. Running stitch the lace to the lower edge of the bottom section.

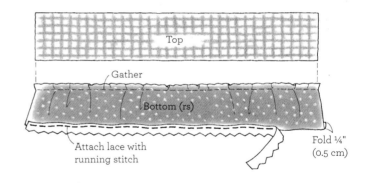

Top
Gather
Bottom (rs)
Attach lace with running stitch
Fold ¼" (0.5 cm)

Align the top and bottom with right sides together and running stitch.

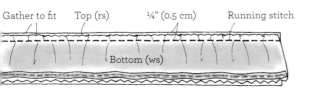

Gather to fit   Top (rs)   ¼" (0.5 cm)   Running stitch
Bottom (ws)

5. Press the seam allowance towards the bottom of the skirt. On the right side, running stitch the lace to the seam.

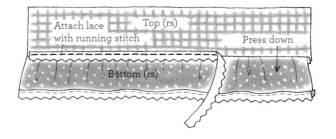

Attach lace with running stitch   Top (rs)   Press down
Bottom (rs)

6. Fold the skirt in half with right sides together and sew along the side. Press the seam allowance open. Fold the waist seam allowance over twice and blind stitch, leaving an opening. Running stitch the waist close to the fold. Insert elastic through waistband and tie to secure. Blind stitch the opening closed, then turn the skirt right side out.

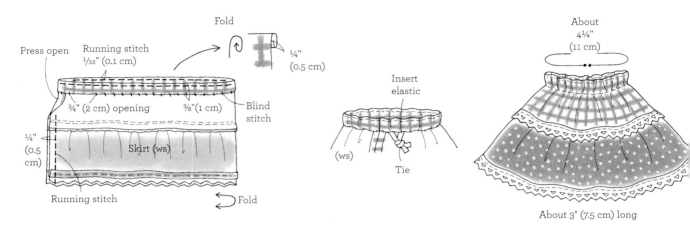

Fold

Press open

Running stitch 1/32" (0.1 cm)

1/4" (0.5 cm)

Insert elastic

About 4¼" (11 cm)

3/4" (2 cm) opening

3/8" (1 cm)

Blind stitch

1/4" (0.5 cm)

Skirt (ws)

(ws)

Tie

Running stitch

Fold

About 3" (7.5 cm) long

8 Floral Gathered Skirt Shown on page 6

Materials

- Floral print cotton fabric: 3¼" x 11¾" (8.5 x 30 cm)
- 11¾" (30 cm) of ½" (1.3 cm) wide pink flower trim
- #25 embroidery floss in white (use 1 strand)
- 6" (15 cm) of ¼" (0.5 cm) wide elastic

There is no template for this project. Refer to the step 1 diagram for cutting dimensions. Seam allowance is included in the skirt cutting dimensions.

1. Fold the skirt in half with right sides together and sew.

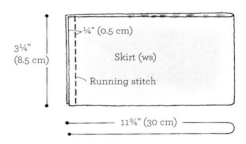

1/4" (0.5 cm)

3¼" (8.5 cm)

Skirt (ws)

Running stitch

11¾" (30 cm)

2. Fold the seam allowance over twice at the waist and the hem. Blind stitch, leaving an opening at the waist. Running stitch the waist close to the fold.

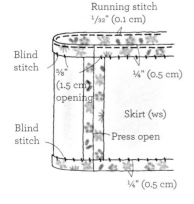

Running stitch 1/32" (0.1 cm)

Blind stitch

5/8" (1.5 cm) opening

1/4" (0.5 cm)

Blind stitch

Skirt (ws)

Press open

1/4" (0.5 cm)

3. Insert elastic through waistband and tie to secure. Blind stitch the opening closed, then turn the skirt right side out. Glue the flower trim to the hem.

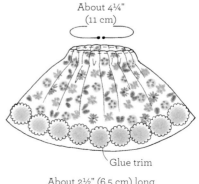

About 4¼" (11 cm)

Glue trim

About 2½" (6.5 cm) long

Jumper Skirt Shown on page 6

Materials

Light blue felt: 4" x 9¾" (10 x 25 cm)

9¾" (25 cm) of ¾" (2 cm) wide Tyrolean ribbon

9¾" (25 cm) of ⅛" (0.3 cm) wide off-white rickrack

9¾" (25 cm) of ¼" (0.7 cm) wide white lace

#25 embroidery floss in light blue and beige (use 1 strand)

6" (15 cm) of ¼" (0.5 cm) wide elastic

There is no template for this project. Refer to the step 1 diagram for cutting dimensions. Seam allowance is included in the skirt cutting dimensions.

1. Blind stitch the ribbon and glue the rickrack and lace to the skirt.

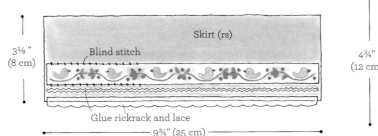

Skirt (rs)
Blind stitch
3⅛" (8 cm)
Glue rickrack and lace
9¾" (25 cm)
Cut 2 suspenders
4¾" (12 cm)
¼" (0.5 cm)

2. Fold the skirt in half with right sides together and sew.

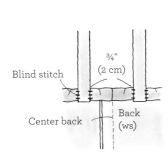

¼" (0.5 cm)
Skirt (ws)
Backstitch

3. Fold the waist seam allowance and blind stitch, leaving an opening.

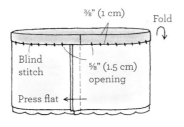

⅜" (1 cm)
Fold
Blind stitch
⅝" (1.5 cm) opening
Press flat

4. Insert elastic through waistband and tie to secure. Blind stitch the opening closed.

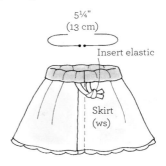

5¼" (13 cm)
Insert elastic
Skirt (ws)

5. Blind stitch the suspenders to the waist on both the front and back. Turn the skirt right side out.

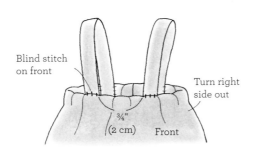

Blind stitch
¾" (2 cm)
Center back
Back (ws)

Blind stitch on front
Turn right side out
¾" (2 cm)
Front

About 2¾" (7 cm) long

10 Linen Slacks & 11 Gingham Pants Shown on page 8

Materials

For Linen Slacks
- Beige linen fabric: 4" x 11¾" (10 x 30 cm)
- #25 embroidery floss in red (use 2 strands)
- Sewing thread in beige
- 6" (15 cm) of ¼" (0.5 cm) wide elastic

For Gingham Pants
- Black and white gingham fabric: 4¾" x 11¾" (12 x 30 cm)
- Sewing thread in white
- 6" (15 cm) of ¼" (0.5 cm) wide elastic

Full-size templates included on page 95.

1. Fold the seam allowance over twice and he the legs on both the front and back.

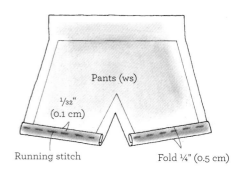

Pants (ws)

¹/₃₂" (0.1 cm)

Running stitch   Fold ¼" (0.5 cm)

2. Align the front and back with right sides together. Sew along sides and inseam.

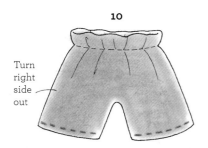

Pants (ws)   (rs)

Leave ¹/₃₂" (0.1 cm)

Clip   Backstitch

3. Press the side seam allowances open. Fold the waist seam allowance and sew, leaving an opening.

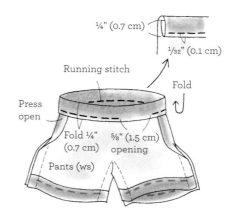

¼" (0.7 cm)

¹/₃₂" (0.1 cm)

Running stitch   Fold

Press open

Fold ¼" (0.7 cm)   ⅝" (1.5 cm) opening

Pants (ws)

4. Insert elastic through waistband and tie to secure. Blind stitch the opening closed.

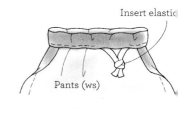

Insert elastic

Pants (ws)

5. Turn right side out.

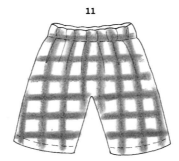

10

Turn right side out

About 2½" (6.5 cm) long

11

About 3" (7.5 cm) long

21 Candy Necklace
Shown on page 10

Materials
- About 60 multi-color raindrop-shaped beads
- About 6¼" (16 cm) of clear elastic line

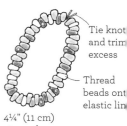

Tie knot and trim excess

Thread beads on elastic line

4¼" (11 cm) circumference

2 Blue Jeans Shown on page 11

Materials
Navy blue felt: 4" x 8" (10 x 20 cm)

#25 embroidery floss in navy blue and white (use 1 strand)

Two ¼" (0.5 cm) diameter pink buttons

One set of ¼" (0.5 cm) diameter snaps

Full-size templates included on page 94.

1. Embroider the front along the sides, hem, and fly.

2. Embroider the back along the sides and hem. Sew the pockets to the back.

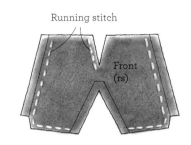

Running stitch

Front (rs)

Running stitch

Back (rs)

Running stitch

3. Align the front and back with right sides together. Sew along sides and inseam.

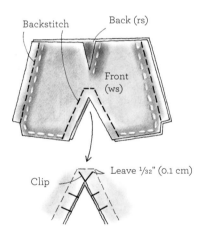

Backstitch

Back (rs)

Front (ws)

Clip

Leave ¹/₃₂" (0.1 cm)

4. Turn right side out. Sew the snaps to the front at the fly and the buttons to the legs.

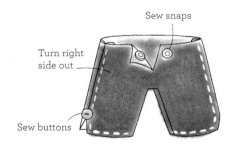

Sew snaps

Turn right side out

Sew buttons

About 2½" (6 cm) long

4 Flower Tote Shown on page 8

Materials
Light green felt: 1½" x 4" (4 x 10 cm)

Red felt: 1½" x 4" (4 x 10 cm)

Scrap of green felt

#25 embroidery floss in light green, red, and white (use 1 strand)

One ⅛" (0.3 cm) diameter yellow button

Full-size templates included on page 92.

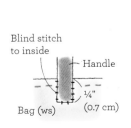

Blind stitch to inside

Handle

Bag (ws)

¼" (0.7 cm)

Sew handle

*Refer to template for embroidery instructions.**

Blanket stitch

Glue and embroider

About 1½" (3.5 cm) long

Country Style   29

13 Matryoshka Bag Shown on page 12

Materials
- Yellow felt: 2" x 3⅛" (5 x 8 cm)
- Blue felt: 1¼" x 3⅛" (3 x 8 cm)
- Scraps of felt in white, beige, red, light brown, and dark brown
- #25 embroidery floss in same colors as felt, plus pink and green (use 1 strand)

Full-size templates included on page 92.

*Refer to templates for embroidery instructions.

Front
Glue
Slip stitch
Back
Slip stitch
Blanket stitch
¼" (0.5 cm)
Hand
Blind

About 1½" (4 cm) long

15 Lace Purse Shown on page 8

Materials
- White felt: 2" x 4" (5 x 10 cm)
- Beige felt: Two ¼" x 2½" (0.5 x 6 cm) pieces
- #25 embroidery floss in white (use 1 strand)
- Two 1¾" (4.5 cm) diameter circles of lace

There is no template for this project.

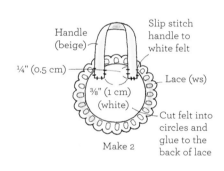

Handle (beige)
Slip stitch handle to white felt
¼" (0.5 cm)
⅜" (1 cm) (white)
Lace (ws)
Cut felt into circles and glue to the back of lace
Make 2

1¾" (4.5 cm) diameter
Backstitch the two pieces together

16 Crochet Cap Shown on page 12

Materials
- Scrap of white medium-weight yarn
- Scrap of white bouclé yarn
- Scrap of multicolor novelty yarn
- ⅜" (1 cm) diameter white pompom
- E/4 (3.5 mm) crochet hook

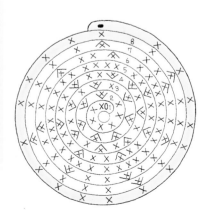

Use medium-weight yarn for rows 1-7 and bouclé yarn for row 8.

Row	Stitches	Increase/Decrease
8	17	Work even
7	17	- 4
6	21	- 7
5	28	Work even
4	28	+ 7 each row
3	21	
2	14	
1	7	Slip knot ring of 7

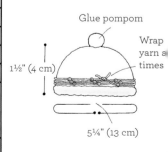

Glue pompom
Wrap yarn a times
1½" (4 cm)
5¼" (13 cm)

7 Lace Headband · Shown on page 9

Materials

½" x 2¾" (1.2 x 7 cm)
of white lace

2¾" (7 cm) of ¼"
(0.5 cm) wide elastic

There is no template for
this project.

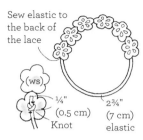

Sew elastic to
the back of
the lace

(ws)

¼"
(0.5 cm)

Knot

2¾"
(7 cm)
elastic

5½" (14 cm) circumference

20 Flower Scarf · Shown on page 11

Materials

- 11" (28 cm) of ⅝" (1.5 cm)
  wide white floral trim

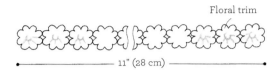

Floral trim

11" (28 cm)

3 Tie Headband · Shown on page 6

Materials

- Pink felt: ¾" x 3⅛" (2 x 8 cm)
- 3" (7.5 cm) of ¼" (0.7 cm) wide white picot ribbon
- 10¼" (26 cm) of ⅛" (0.3 cm) wide white rickrack
- Two white flower motifs
- Two silver beads

A full-size template is included on page 94.

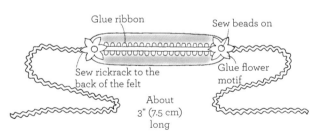

Glue ribbon

Sew beads on

Sew rickrack to the
back of the felt

Glue flower
motif

About
3" (7.5 cm)
long

19 Detachable Collar · Shown on page 10

Materials

- White felt: 2½" x 4" (6 x 10 cm)
- 15¾" (40 cm) of ⅛" (0.3 cm) wide red rickrack

A full-size template is included on page 94.

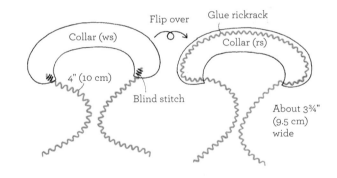

Flip over

Glue rickrack

Collar (ws)

Collar (rs)

4" (10 cm)

Blind stitch

About 3¾"
(9.5 cm)
wide

22 Boo the Bear · Shown on page 11

Materials

- Brown felt: 3⅛" x 6" (8 x 15 cm)
- Scraps of white, light brown, dark
  brown, and blue felt
- #25 embroidery floss in light brown,
  brown, and white (use 1 strand)
- Three ⅛" (0.3 cm) diameter buttons
  (2 pink and 1 blue)
- Stuffing

Full-size templates included on page 94.

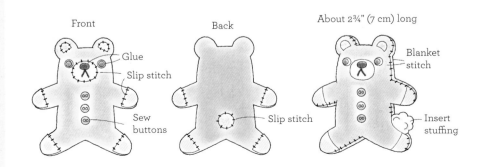

Front

Back

About 2¾" (7 cm) long

Glue

Slip stitch

Sew
buttons

Slip stitch

Blanket
stitch

Insert
stuffing

Collection 2:

Uptown Girls

Meet our cute dark-eyed beauties.
They love elegant, ladylike clothes with touches of lace and pearls.
These girls can't wait to get out and be seen around town.

28 + 30

27 + 32

Meet the Dolls

Laura
Favorite Color: Red
Favorite Accessory: Pink hair ribbon
Trademark: Classic bun

Instructions on page 38

Lily
Favorite Color: White
Favorite Accessory: White shoulder bag
Trademark: Straight bangs

Instructions on page 38

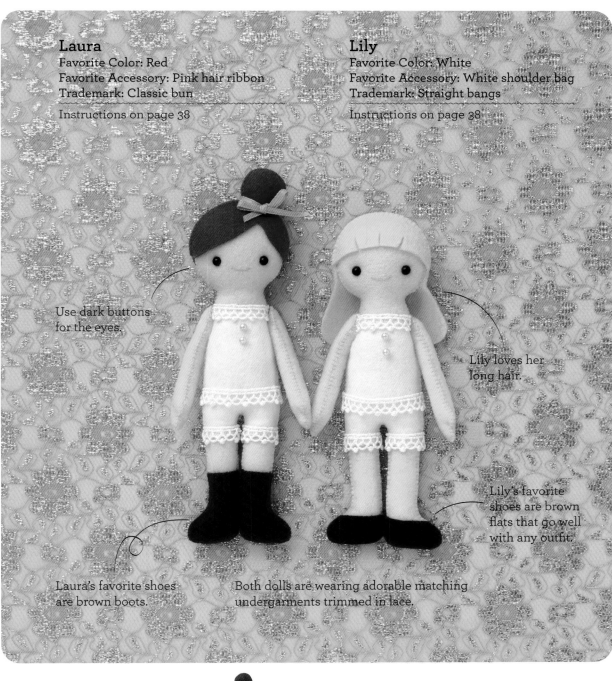

Use dark buttons
for the eyes.

Lily loves her
long hair.

Lily's favorite
shoes are brown
flats that go well
with any outfit.

Laura's favorite shoes
are brown boots.

Both dolls are wearing adorable matching
undergarments trimmed in lace.

*This collection is designed and
handmade by Chibirobin.*

Back View

Outfit Ideas

Laura and Lily have a tasteful, stylish wardrobe with a lot of mix and match options! Here are a few outfit ideas for all different occasions.

25 + 34

The brown Pochette (34) makes a striking addition to the red Shift Dress trimmed in lace (25).

27 + 31 + 33

Lily looks comfortable in her brown Cargo Pants (31) and Peasant Blouse (27). The white Shoulder Bag (33) is the perfect accessory.

23 + 27 + 32

Laura is cute and stylish in her Rolled Cuff Capris (32) and Peasant Blouse (27). The Camel Hair Coat (23) makes the perfect outerwear; she's ready for a walk in the park.

24 + 28 + 29

Try coordinating the turquoise Sleeveless Shell (28) with the pink Pleated Skirt (29). Layer the ensemble with the white Waist-Length Jacket (24) for a ladylike look.

Take me with you!

26

nmed in rickrack and floral ribbon, Laura's blue Sundress (26) is the perfect outfit for a summer day. The mascot strap great addition and transforms Laura into a key chain. Now she can go wherever you go!

Attach a key chain to the back using a piece of ribbon.

Laura and Lily's Wardrobe

Outerwear

23
Camel Hair Coat
Instructions on page 41

24
Waist-Length Jacket
Instructions on page 42

Tops and Dresses

Back View

25
Shift Dress
Instructions on page 43

This dress buttons
down the back

Back View

26
Sundress
Instructions on page 43

The pleats continue on
the back of the dress

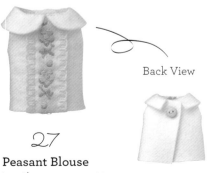

Back View

27
Peasant Blouse
Instructions on page 44

The blouse closes
with a single button
at the back

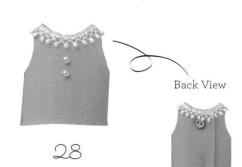

Back View

28
Sleeveless Shell
Instructions on page 44

The lace adds a
special touch to the
back neckline

rts and Pants

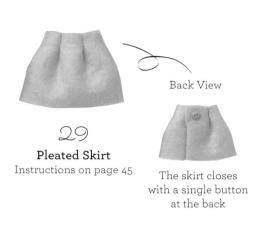

29
Pleated Skirt
Instructions on page 45

Back View

The skirt closes
with a single button
at the back

30
Wrap Skirt
Instructions on page 46

31
Cargo Pants
Instructions on page 46

Back View

Add a patch pocket
on the back

32
Rolled Cuff Capris
Instructions on page 46

Back View

Topstitch the
pocket with con-
trasting thread

gs

33
Shoulder Bag
Instructions on page 47

34
Pochette
Instructions on page 47

Laura and Lily Shown on page 32

Materials (makes 1 doll)

Felt
- Peach: 4" x 8" (10 x 20 cm)
- White: 2¾" x 4" (7 x 10 cm)
- Dark brown: 2" x 2¾" (5 x 7 cm)
- Reddish brown (for Laura): 2¾" x 4" (7 x 10 cm)
- Light yellow (for Lily): 2¾" x 4" (7 x 10 cm)

Notions
- #25 embroidery floss in the same colors as felt, plus pink (use 1 strand)
- ⅛" (0.3 cm) wide pink satin ribbon (for Laura)
- Two ⅛" (0.3 cm) diameter pearl beads
- Two ¼" (0.4 cm) diameter black eye buttons
- 11¾" (30 cm) of ⅜" (0.8 cm wide) white lace
- Stuffing

Cutting Instructions

Trace and cut out the full-size templates on page 97. Pin or tape the templates to the felt and cut out following the instructions listed on the templates.

1. Make the body

a. Align the body with the head and attach using slip stitch. Follow the same process to attach the legs to the body and the shoes to the legs. Repeat process for the back. Sew the two pearl beads to the camisole on the front.

b. Align the front and back, then sew together using blanket stitch, inserting the stuffing as you work.

c. Wrap the lace around the neckline, waist, and legs. Slip stitch the lace to the felt. Overlap the short ends and glue.

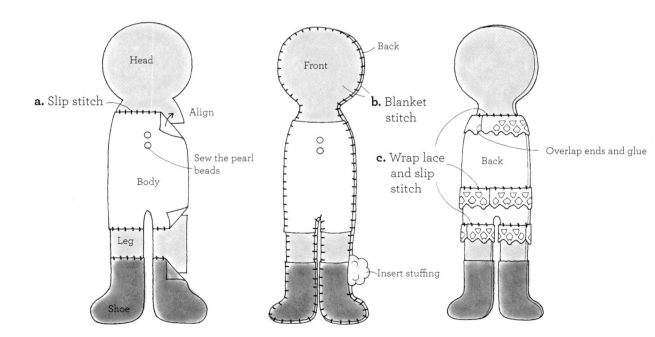

Make the arms

Align two arms and sew together using blanket stitch, inserting the stuffing as you work. Repeat for the other arm.

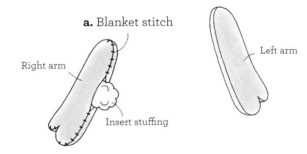

a. Blanket stitch

Left arm

Right arm

Insert stuffing

Make the face

Use a stiletto to puncture a small hole at the position to attach each eye.

Starting from the back, sew each eye button to the head, pulling tightly to make a small indent and to bring the base of the eye button inside the head.

Embroider the mouth following the instructions on the head template. Leave a bit of slack in the thread and secure with glue.

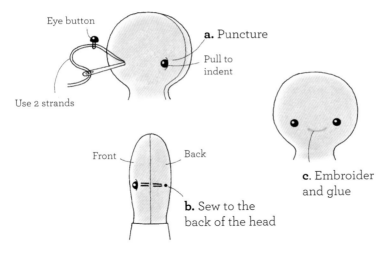

Eye button

a. Puncture

Pull to indent

Use 2 strands

Front   Back

b. Sew to the back of the head

c. Embroider and glue

Attach the hair

Align the front and back hair pieces with right sides facing out and blanket stitch together. For Lily, clip the front hair to make bangs.

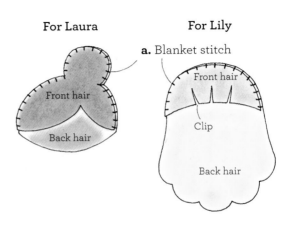

For Laura   For Lily

a. Blanket stitch

Front hair

Front hair

Clip

Back hair

Back hair

5. Finish the dolls

a. Glue the hair to the head. For Laura, insert stuffing into the bun before gluing the hair to the head. Wrap the ribbon around the bun and tie a bow.

b. To attach the arms, make a knot and stitch into the side seam. Insert the needle through the body and arms as indicated by the dotted line in the diagram below. Knot the thread to secure.

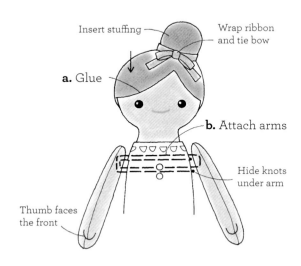

Insert stuffing

Wrap ribbon and tie bow

a. Glue

b. Attach arms

Hide knots under arm

Thumb faces the front

Laura

Lily

5½" (14 cm) tall

3 Camel Hair Coat Shown on page 34

Materials

- Beige felt: 8" x 8" (20 x 20 cm)
- #25 embroidery floss in beige (use 1 strand)
- 13¾" (35 cm) of ⅜" (0.9 cm) wide white lace
- Two ¼" (0.6 cm) diameter white buttons

Full-size templates included on page 100.

Running stitch the lace to the neckline and hems. Make buttonholes and attach buttons.

2. Fold the coat with right sides together. Sew along the sides. Fold each sleeve with right sides together and sew, stopping at the mark.

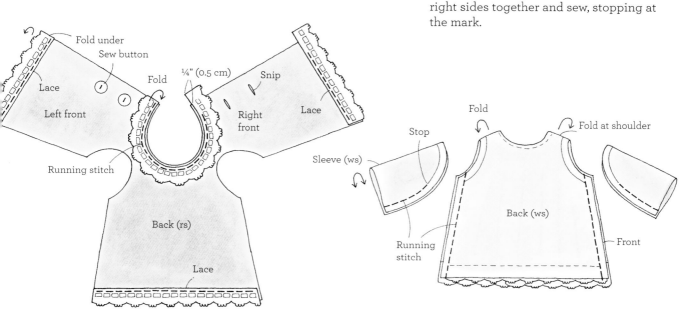

Turn the sleeve right side out. Insert the sleeve into the armhole with right sides together. Sew around the armhole. Repeat for the other sleeve.

4. Turn the coat right side out. Fold up the sleeve cuffs.

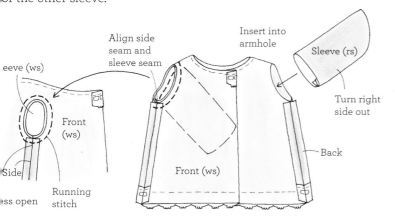

Materials

- White felt: 4¼" x 6¼" (11 x 16 cm)
- #25 embroidery floss in white (use 1 strand)
- 4" (10 cm) of ⅜" (0.8 cm) wide white lace

Full-size templates included on page 101.

1. Sew the lace to the center front edges.

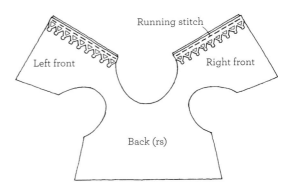

2. Fold the jacket with right sides together. Sew along the sides. Press the seam allowances open. Fold each sleeve with right sides together and sew, stopping at the mark.

3. Turn the sleeve right side out. Insert the sleeve into the armhole with right sides together. Sew around the armhole. Repeat for the other sleeve.

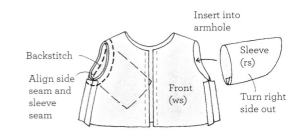

4. Turn the jacket right side out.

About 2¼" (5.5 cm) long

25 Shift Dress Shown on page 34

Materials

- Red felt: 4¾" x 8" (12 x 20 cm)
- #25 embroidery floss in red and white (use 1 strand)
- 11¾" (30 cm) of ⅜" (0.9 cm) wide white lace
- 7" (18 cm) of ⅛" (0.3 cm) wide brown satin ribbon
- Two ¼" (0.7 cm) diameter white buttons

Full-size template included on page 98.

1. Sew lace to the hems. Sew lace to the front, gathering as shown in the diagram. Cut ribbon in half and sew to the front. Make buttonholes and attach buttons.

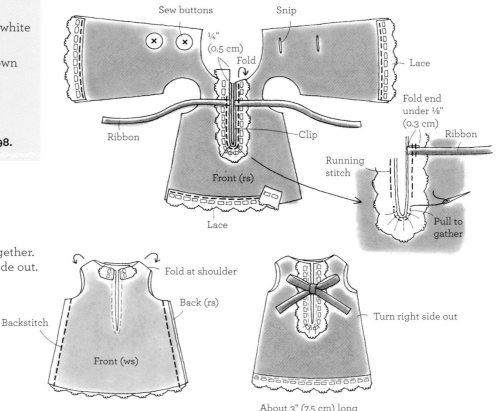

Sew buttons   Snip
¼" (0.5 cm)
Fold
Lace
Fold end under ⅛" (0.3 cm)
Ribbon
Ribbon
Clip
Running stitch
Front (rs)
Lace
Pull to gather

2. Fold the dress with right sides together. Sew along the sides. Turn right side out.

Fold at shoulder
Back (rs)
Backstitch
Turn right side out
Front (ws)
About 3" (7.5 cm) long

26 Sundress Shown on page 35

Materials

- Light blue felt: 4¾" x 8" (12 x 20 cm)
- #25 embroidery floss in light blue (use 1 strand)
- 2" (5 cm) of ¾" (1.8 cm) wide Tyrolean ribbon
- 8" (20 cm) of ⅛" (0.3 cm) wide light blue rickrack
- Two ¼" (0.6 cm) diameter white buttons

Full-size templates included on page 99.

1. Sew the rickrack to the skirt. Fold and sew the six pleats following placement indicated on the template.

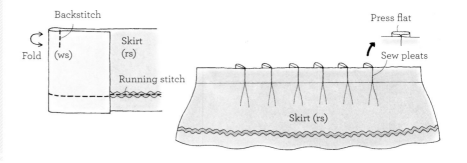

Backstitch
Press flat
Fold   (ws)   Skirt (rs)
Sew pleats
Running stitch
Skirt (rs)

2. Sew the ribbon to the front bodice following placement indicated on template. Align bodice on top of skirt and backstitch. Make buttonholes and attach buttons.

3. Overlap the front and back bodice at the shoulders and slip stitch.

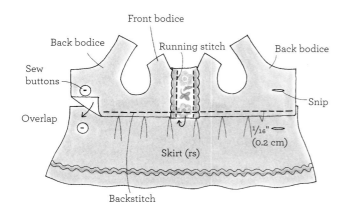

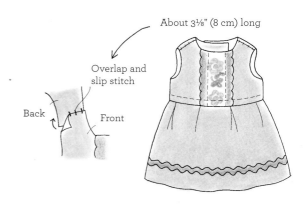

27 Peasant Blouse and 28 Sleeveless Shell Shown on page 32

Materials

For Peasant Blouse
- White felt: 3½" x 5¼" (9 x 13 cm)
- #25 embroidery floss in white (use 1 strand)
- 2½" (6 cm) of ¾" (1.8 cm) wide Tyrolean ribbon
- One ¼" (0.6 cm) diameter pink button

For Sleeveless Shell
- Turquoise felt: 3⅛" x 5¼" (8 x 13 cm)
- #25 embroidery floss in turquoise (use 1 strand)
- 4" (10 cm) of ⅜" (0.8 cm) wide white lace
- Two ⅛" (0.3 cm) diameter pearl beads
- One ¼" (0.6 cm) diameter white button

Full-size templates included on page 101.

1. Running stitch the ribbon to the front.

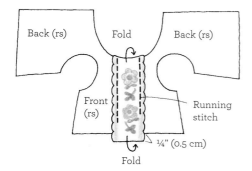

2. For the Peasant Blouse, align the two collar pieces with the neckline and blanket stitch. For both shirts, make buttonhole and attach the button.

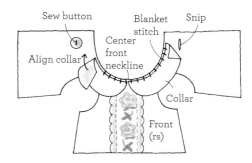

Fold the shirt with right sides together. Sew along the sides.

4. Turn right side out. For the Sleeveless Blouse, sew the lace to the neckline and sew the pearl beads to the front.

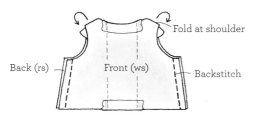

Back (rs) — Front (ws) — Backstitch

Fold at shoulder

27

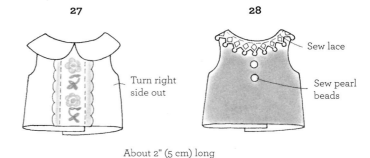

Turn right side out

28

Sew lace

Sew pearl beads

About 2" (5 cm) long

29 Pleated Skirt Shown on page 34

Shown on page 34

Materials
- Light pink felt: 2½" x 6¾" (6 x 17 cm)
- #25 embroidery floss in light pink (use 1 strand)
- One ¼" (0.6 cm) diameter pink button

Full-size template included on page 99.

1. With right sides together, fold and sew the five pleats following placement indicated on the template. Make a buttonhole and attach the button.

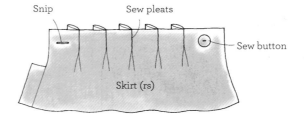

Snip

Sew pleats

Sew button

Skirt (rs)

Fold the skirt in half with right sides together and backstitch, as shown in the diagram below. Turn the skirt right side out.

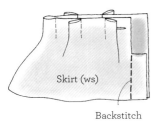

Skirt (ws)

Backstitch

About 2" (5 cm) long

30 Wrap Skirt Shown on page 32

Materials

- Turquoise felt: 3⅛" x 7" (8 x 18 cm)
- Sewing thread in white
- 8" (20 cm) of ⅜" (0.8 cm) wide white lace
- One ¼" (0.6 cm) diameter white button

Full-size template included on page 98.

1. Running stitch the lace to the hem. Make a buttonhole and attach the button.

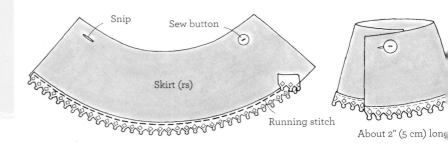

31 Cargo Pants and 32 Rolled Cuff Capris Shown on pages 32 and 34

Materials

For Cargo Pants
- Beige felt: 2¾" x 8" (7 x 20 cm)
- #25 embroidery floss in beige (use 1 strand)

For Rolled Cuff Capris
- Blue felt: 3⅛" x 8" (8 x 20 cm)
- #25 embroidery floss in blue and beige (use 1 strand)

Full-size templates included on pages 100 and 101.

1. Backstitch the pocket to the right leg. Use beige embroidery floss for both pairs of pants.

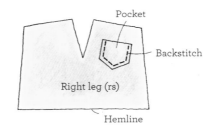

2. With right sides together, sew the right and left legs along the V-shaped inseam.

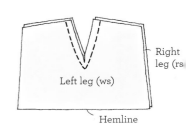

3. Press the inseam seam allowance open. Turn right side out.

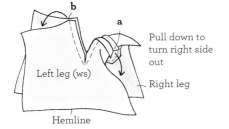

4. Fold each leg with right sides together, aligning **a** and **b**.

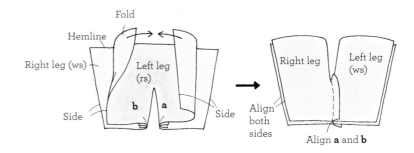

Backstitch along the sides.

6. Turn right side out. For the Rolled Cuff Capris, fold up the pant cuffs.

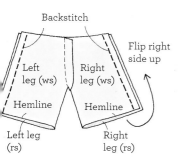

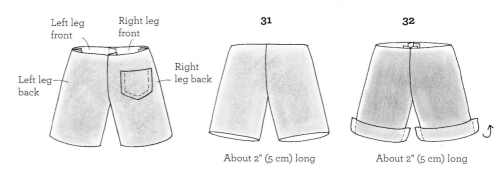

33 *Shoulder Bag* and 34 *Pochette* Shown on page 34

Materials

For Shoulder Bag

White felt: 2" x 3⅛" (5 x 8 cm)

#25 embroidery floss in white (use 1 strand)

½" (1.2 cm) lace flower motif

7" (18 cm) of 1/32" (0.1 cm) diameter white cord

One metal charm

One ⅛" (0.3 cm) diameter pearl bead

Full-size templates included on page 101.

For Pochette

- Dark brown felt: 2" x 3⅛" (5 x 8 cm)
- #25 embroidery floss in dark brown (use 1 strand)
- 1" x 1¼" (2.5 x 3 cm) oval lace motif
- 7" (18 cm) of 1/32" (0.1 cm) diameter dark brown cord
- One metal charm
- One ¼" (0.5 cm) diameter snap set

For Shoulder Bag

Blanket stitch front and back together with right sides facing out. Make buttonhole and attach pearl bead. Make holes. Thread charm onto cord, insert through holes, and knot. Sew lace to flap.

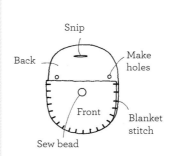

About 1" (2.5 cm) long

Pochette

Sew the snap components to the front and back. Running stitch front to back. Blanket stitch front and back together with right sides facing out. Make holes. Thread charm onto cord, insert through holes, and knot.

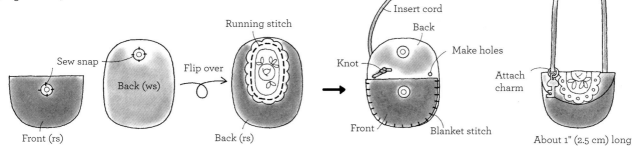

About 1" (2.5 cm) long

Collection 3:

Preppy Pals

Meet our cute preppy pals, Lydia and Amelia. They
adore vintage clothes and love wearing retro fashions.
They can't wait to share those styles with you!

42 + 47

43 + 46 + 49

Meet the Dolls

Lydia
Eye Color: Blue
Favorite Garment:
Hooded Cape

Instructions on page 56

Use embroidery stitches to create realistic-looking strands of hair.

Lydia wears comfortable, practical lace-up boots.

Amelia
Eye Color: Brown
Favorite Garment: Frilly Dress

Instructions on page 56

Their arms are attached with snaps, making for quick and easy outfit changes.

Amelia's beaded ballet slippers make any outfit more formal.

Back View

This collection is designed and handmade by Kaori Shimazu.

Outfit Ideas

After making the dolls, have fun sewing their clothes! The more clothes you make, the more outfits you can create!

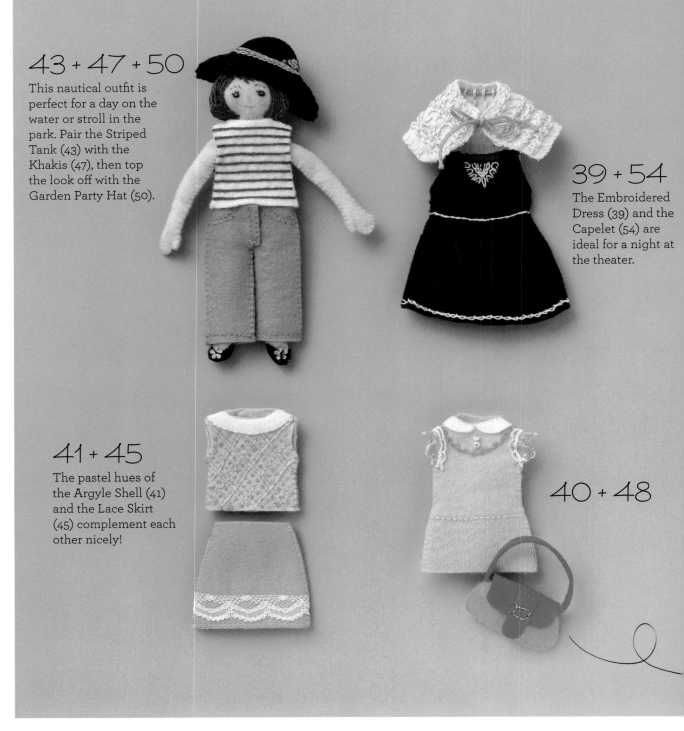

43 + 47 + 50

This nautical outfit is perfect for a day on the water or stroll in the park. Pair the Striped Tank (43) with the Khakis (47), then top the look off with the Garden Party Hat (50).

39 + 54

The Embroidered Dress (39) and the Capelet (54) are ideal for a night at the theater.

41 + 45

The pastel hues of the Argyle Shell (41) and the Lace Skirt (45) complement each other nicely!

40 + 48

For more about the clothes and accessories shown on the left and below, see pages 54-55.

This is my favorite handbag!

40 + 48

The retro-inspired Frilly Dress (40) features a variety of pretty and feminine details. Embroider the skirt to create a pleated effect. Complete the look with the Buckle Purse (48) and Lydia is ready for a night on the town!

42 + 44 + 53

The Ruffle Sleeve Blouse (42) and the Maxi Skirt (44) coordinate well. Add the Rosette Collar (53) for a vintage touch.

36 + 47 + 51 + 52

Bundle your doll up on those cold, snowy days! She'll stay warm and cozy in the Pea Coat (36) and Khakis (47). T colorful embellishment on t Cloche (51) matches the col of the Crochet Scarf (52).

35 + 46 + 52 + 56

This outfit is perfect for outdoor activities like hiking. Throw the Hooded Cape (35) over the Camp Shorts (46), then add the Crochet Scarf (52) and Wool Mittens (56) if Lydia gets chilly.

37 + 43 + 45

For a classic look, combine the Camel Blazer (37), Striped Tank (43), and the Lace Skirt (45).

For more about the clothes and accessories shown on the left and below, see pages 54-55.

I'm ready to paint the town!

38 + 39 + 55

Amelia is dressed to the nines! For a formal occasion, combine the Embroidered Dress (39) and Collarless Jacket (38), then accessorize with the Beaded Necklace (55).

Lydia & Amelia's Wardrobe

Outerwear

35
Hooded Cape
Instructions on page 59

36
Pea Coat
Instructions on page 60

Back View

Add two beads to the back tab for a special detail

37
Camel Blazer
Instructions on page 62

38
Collarless Jacket
Instructions on page 63

Tops & Dresses

39
Embroidered Dress
Instructions on page 64

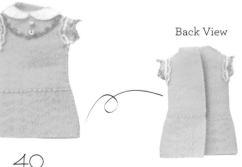

40
Frilly Dress
Instructions on page 65

Back View

Don't forget to embroider pleats on the back too

41
Argyle Shell
Instructions on page 65

42
Ruffle Sleeve Blouse
Instructions on page 66

43
Striped Tank
Instructions on page 67

ottoms

44
Maxi Skirt
Instructions on page 68

45
Lace Skirt
Instructions on page 61

46
Camp Shorts
Instructions on page 61

Back View

Embroider
the pockets
on the back

47
Khakis
Instructions on page 68

Back View

Add pleats on
the back waist

Bags

48
Buckle Purse
Instructions on page 70

49
Pocket Tote
Instructions on page 71

cessories

50
Garden Party Hat
Instructions on page 58

51
Cloche
Instructions on page 59

52
Crochet Scarves
Instructions on page 69

53
Rosette Collar
Instructions on page 66

54
Capelet
Instructions on page 69

55
Beaded Necklace
Instructions on page 71

56
Wool Mittens
Instructions on page 70

Materials (makes 1 doll)

Felt
- Peach: 6" x 7" (15 x 18 cm)
- Beige (for Lydia): 2" x 3½" (5 x 9 cm)

Fabric
- Muslin: 2½" x 4" (6 x 10 cm)

Notions
- #25 embroidery floss in peach, beige, navy blue, black, white, brown, and pink (use 1 strand)
- Two ¼" (0.5 cm) diameter snaps
- Two blue flower-shaped sequins (for Amelia)
- Stuffing
- Blush

Cutting Instructions

Trace and cut out the full-size templates on page 102. Pin or tape the templates to the felt and cut out following the instructions listed on the templates.

1. Make the body

a. Align the front and back, then sew together using blanket stitch, inserting the stuffing as you work.

2. Embroider Amelia's hair, face, and shoes

a. Outline stitch the hair without leaving space between the stitches. Embroider the eyes, nose, and mouth following instructions on the body template. Add a dab of blush for the cheeks.

b. Embroider the straps following the instructions on the body template.

c. Outline stitch the shoes.

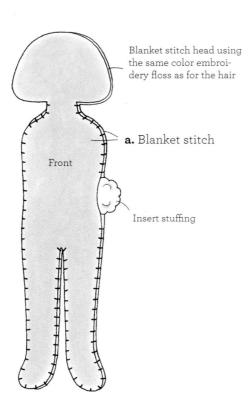

Blanket stitch head using the same color embroidery floss as for the hair

a. Blanket stitch

Front

Insert stuffing

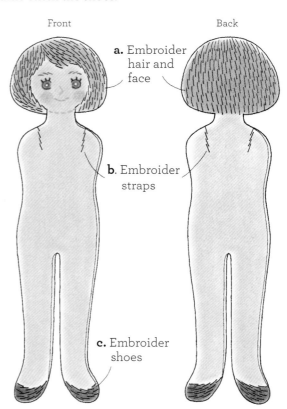

Front

Back

a. Embroider hair and face

b. Embroider straps

c. Embroider shoes

Make the arms (for both Lydia and Amelia)

Align two arm pieces and sew together using blanket stitch, inserting the stuffing as you work. Repeat for the other arm.

Sew the female snap components to the body and the male snap components to the arms.

Blanket stitch the camisole pieces to the body using 2 strands of white embroidery floss.

Cable chain stitch along the neckline and waistline of the camisole using 2 strands of white embroidery floss. Embroider both the front and back.

For Amelia only, sew the flower-shaped sequins to the shoes.

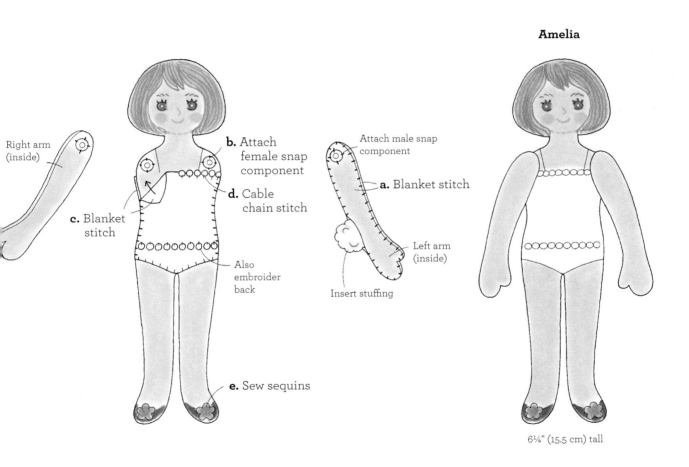

Right arm (inside)

b. Attach female snap component

Attach male snap component

a. Blanket stitch

d. Cable chain stitch

c. Blanket stitch

Also embroider back

Left arm (inside)

Insert stuffing

e. Sew sequins

Amelia

6¼" (15.5 cm) tall

4. Finish Lydia

a. Outline stitch the hair without leaving space between the stitches. Embroider spirals at the ends to create curls. Embroider the eyes, nose, and mouth following the instructions on the body template. Add a dab of blush for the cheeks. Embroider the straps following instructions on the body template.

b. Blanket stitch the shoes to the feet.

c. Slip stitch the top of the shoes to the legs.

d. Embroider the shoelaces.

Lydia

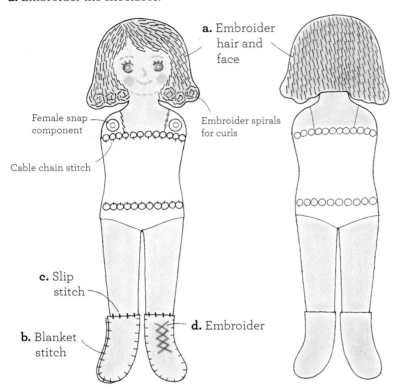

a. Embroider hair and face

Female snap component

Embroider spirals for curls

Cable chain stitch

c. Slip stitch

d. Embroider

b. Blanket stitch

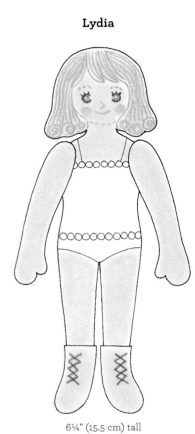

6¼" (15.5 cm) tall

50 Garden Party Hat Shown on page 50

Materials
- Navy blue felt: 2" x 6" (5 x 15 cm)
- #25 embroidery floss in navy blue, pink, green, and light green (use 1 strand)

Full-size templates included on page 109.

* **Refer to template for embroidery instructions.**

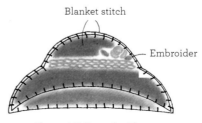

Blanket stitch

Embroider

About 2½" (6.5 cm) wide

Materials

Heather gray felt: 6" x 8" (15 x 20 cm)

#25 embroidery floss in light blue (use 3 strands)

One ¼" (0.6 cm) diameter blue bead

All-size templates included on page 108.

1. Align the two hood pieces. Blanket stitch together, then continue sewing along the remaining raw edges of the back hood. Align the front and back pieces. Blanket stitch together along the sides, then continue sewing along the remaining raw edges. Make a buttonhole and attach the bead.

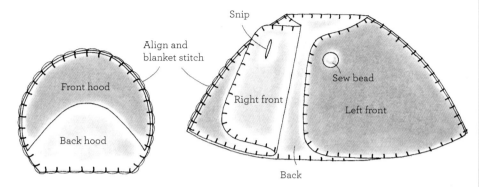

2. Blanket stitch the hood to the back.

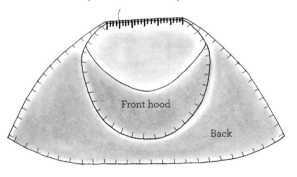

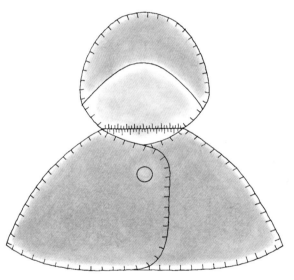

About 2½" (6.5 cm) long

Materials

Heather gray felt: 1½" x 4¾" (4 x 12 cm)

#25 embroidery floss in gray (use 1 strand)

Two clover-shaped sequins

All-size templates included on page 103.

* Refer to template for embroidery instructions.

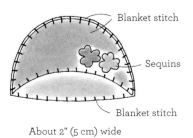

About 2" (5 cm) wide

36 Pea Coat Shown on page 52

Materials

- Red felt: 8" x 8" (20 x 20 cm)
- #25 embroidery floss in red (use 1 strand)
- One ¼" (0.5 cm) diameter snap
- Ten brown beads

Full-size templates included on page 107.

1. Running stitch the collar, then blanket stitch the collar to the neckline. Running stitch the pockets to the front and the tab to the back.

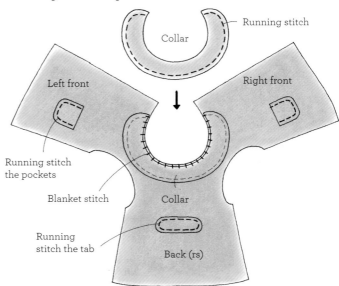

Running stitch — Collar

Left front — Right front

Running stitch the pockets

Blanket stitch — Collar

Running stitch the tab

Back (rs)

2. Fold the cuff up on each sleeve and running stitch. Sew each sleeve to the body, as shown in step 2 on page 63.

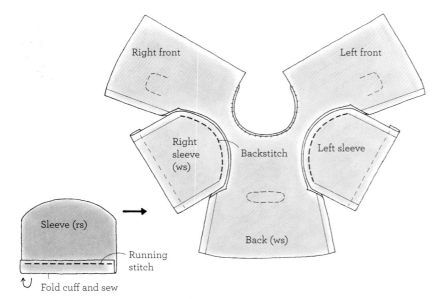

Right front — Left front

Right sleeve (ws) — Backstitch — Left sleeve

Sleeve (rs)

Running stitch

Fold cuff and sew

Back (ws)

3. Fold the sleeve in half at the shoulder. Start at the bottom hem, sew the front and back together. Continue sewing the sleeve toget making sure not to stitch through the sean allowance. Stop sewing at the sleeve hem.

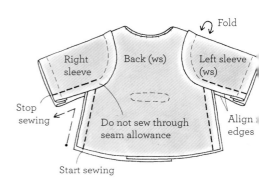

Fold

Right sleeve — Back (ws) — Left sleeve (ws)

Stop sewing

Do not sew through seam allowance

Align edges

Start sewing

4. Turn the coat right side out. Sew eight beads to right front. Sew the snap components to the front.

5. Sew two beads to the back tab.

Sew snap

Sew beads

Sew beads

About 3" (7.5 cm) long

5 Lace Skirt Shown on page 50

Shown on page 50

Materials

Light blue felt: 2½" x 6" (6 x 15 cm)

#25 embroidery floss in light blue (use 1 strand)

One ¼" x ⅝" (0.5 x 1.5 cm) piece of hook-and-loop tape

6" (15 cm) of ½" (1.2 cm) wide white lace

Full-size templates included on page 103.

1. Blanket stitch front and back pieces together at sides. Blanket stitch the hem. Slip stitch the hook-and-loop tape to the back pieces. Running stitch the lace to the bottom of the skirt.

Slip stitch

Blanket stitch

Left back

Right back

Blanket stitch hem

Front

About 2" (5 cm) long

Running stitch

6 Camp Shorts Shown on page 48

Shown on page 48

Materials

Olive green felt: 2" x 5¼" (5 x 13 cm)

#25 embroidery floss in olive green (use 1 strand)

Full-size templates included on page 105.

1. Embroider following instructions on template. Blanket stitch front and back together at sides and inseam.

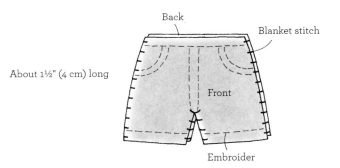

Back

Blanket stitch

About 1½" (4 cm) long

Front

Embroider

37 Camel Blazer Shown on page 52

Materials
- Beige felt: 5¼" x 8" (13 x 20 cm)
- #25 embroidery floss in beige (use 1 strand)
- Four ⅛" (0.3 cm) diameter wooden beads

Full-size templates included on page 106.

1. Blanket stitch the collar to the neckline. Running stitch the pockets to the front.

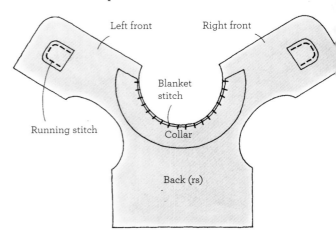

2. Sew each sleeve to the body, as shown in step 2 on page 63.

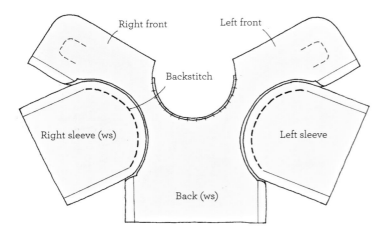

3. Fold the sleeve in half at the shoulder. Starting at the bottom hem, sew the front and back together. Continue sewing the sleeve together, making sure not to stitch through the seam allowance. Stop sewing at the sleeve hem.

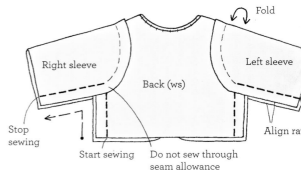

4. Turn the blazer right side out. Sew the buttons to the right front.

About 2¼" (5.5 cm) long

3 Collarless Jacket Shown on page 53

Materials

White felt: 4" x 8" (10 x 20 cm)

#25 embroidery floss in white and navy blue (use 1 strand)

Full-size templates included on page 106.

1. Embroider the body and sleeves following instructions on templates. Running stitch the pockets to the front. With right sides together, align each sleeve with the body at the shoulder.

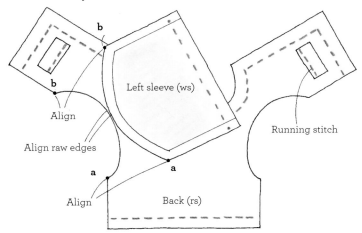

Align marks **a** and **b** on the sleeve and the body. Sew the sleeve to the body, easing the fullness of the sleeve into the curve of the armhole. Repeat for the remaining sleeve.

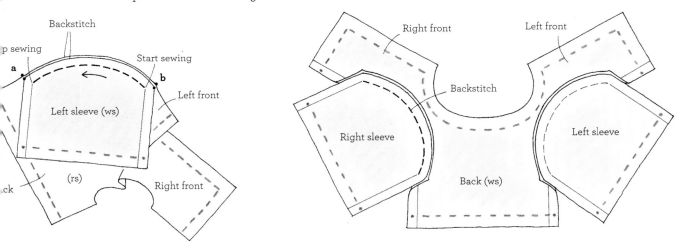

Fold the sleeve in half at the shoulder. Starting at the bottom hem, sew the front and back together. Continue sewing the sleeve together, making sure not to stitch through the seam allowance. Stop sewing at the sleeve hem. Turn the jacket right side out.

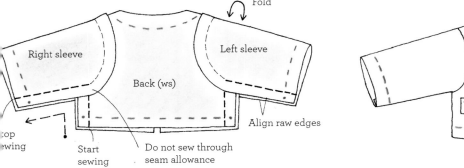

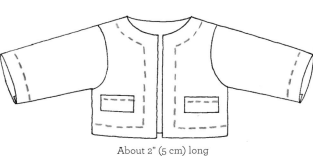

About 2" (5 cm) long

39 *Embroidered Dress* Shown on page 50

Materials

- Navy blue felt: 2¾" x 4¾" (7 x 12 cm)
- #25 embroidery floss in navy blue and white (use 1 strand)
- One ⅜" x ⅜" (1 x 1 cm) piece of hook-and-loop tape

Full-size templates included on page 105.

1. Embroider the front bodice and both skirt pieces following the instructions on the templates. Fold the pleats on the skirt and slip stitch.

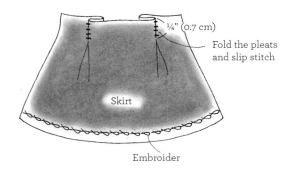

¼" (0.7 cm)

Fold the pleats and slip stitch

Skirt

Embroider

2. Slip stitch the straps to the front bodice and the front bodice to a skirt piece. Cut the hook-and-loop tape in half. Slip stitch the loop side of the tape (the soft half) to the wrong side of each strap.

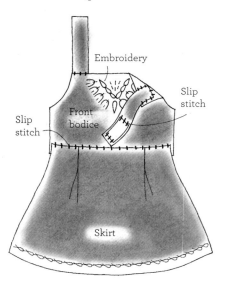

Embroidery

Slip stitch

Front bodice

Slip stitch

Skirt

3. Slip stitch the back bodice to the other skirt piece. Slip stitch the hook side of the tape (the stiff half) to the right side of the back bodice.

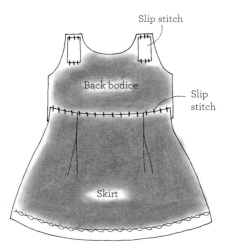

Slip stitch

Back bodice

Slip stitch

Skirt

4. Blanket stitch the front and back together along the sid

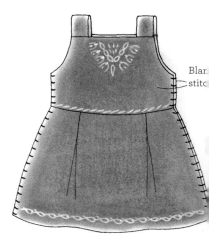

Blan stitc

About 3½" (9 cm) long

O Frilly Dress Shown on page 50

Shown on page 50

Materials

Pink felt: 3½" x 6" (9 x 15 cm)

White felt: ¾" x 1½" (2 x 4 cm)

#25 embroidery floss in light pink, pink, and white (use 1 strand)

4" (10 cm) of ⅜" (1 cm) wide pink lace

One ⅜" x 1" (1 x 2.5 cm) piece of hook-and-loop tape

Two round white beads

Full-size templates included on page 109.

1. Embroider the neckline on the front, then embroider the pleats on the front and both back pieces following instructions on templates. Blanket stitch the collar to the front.

Blanket stitch

2. Align the front and back pieces. Blanket stitch together along the shoulders and sides. Running stitch the lace to the armholes. Cut the hook-and-loop tape in half and slip stitch to the back pieces. Sew the beads to the front.

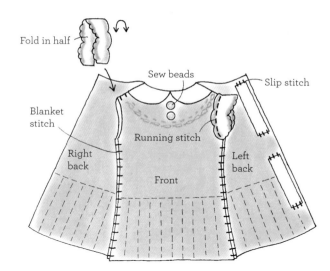

Fold in half

Sew beads

Slip stitch

Blanket stitch

Running stitch

Right back

Left back

Front

About 3" (7.5 cm) long

Argyle Shell Shown on page 50

Shown on page 50

Materials

Pink felt: 2" x 6" (5 x 15 cm)

White felt: ¾" x 2" (2 x 5 cm)

#25 embroidery floss in pink, yellow, light blue, light green, and white (use 1 strand)

One ¼" x 1" (0.5 x 2.5 cm) piece of hook-and-loop tape

Full-size templates included on page 103.

1. Embroider the front and back pieces following the instructions on the templates. Slip stitch the collar to the front.

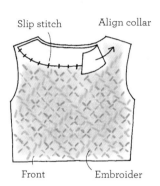

Slip stitch

Align collar

Front

Embroider

2. Blanket stitch the front and back pieces together along the shoulders and sides. Slip stitch the hook-and-loop tape to the back pieces.

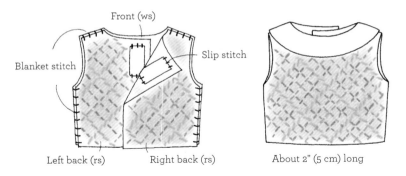

Front (ws)

Blanket stitch

Slip stitch

Left back (rs)   Right back (rs)

About 2" (5 cm) long

53 Rosette Collar   Shown on page 52

Materials
- White felt: 2" x 4¾" (5 x 12 cm)
- #25 embroidery floss in white, pink, and green (use 1 strand)
- One ⅛" (0.3 cm) diameter red bead
- Mini elastic band

Full-size templates included on page 108.

* **Refer to template for embroidery instructions.**

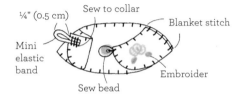

¼" (0.5 cm)   Sew to collar
                                Blanket stitch
Mini
elastic
band
                                Embroider
Sew bead

About 1¾" (4.5 cm) wide

42 Ruffle Sleeve Blouse   Shown on page 48

Materials
- Yellow felt: 2" x 6¼" (5 x 16 cm)
- #25 embroidery floss in yellow (use 1 strand)
- One ¼" x 1" (0.5 x 2.5 cm) piece of hook-and-loop tape
- Three round gold beads

Full-size templates included on page 105.

1. Running stitch and gather the sleeves.

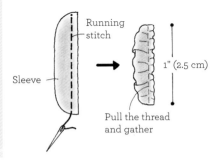

Running stitch

Sleeve

1" (2.5 cm)

Pull the thread and gather

2. Embroider the front following instructions on template. Blanket stitch the back pieces to the front along the shoulders. Position each sleeve underneath the body and slip stitch. Slip stitch the hook-and-loop tape to the back pieces.

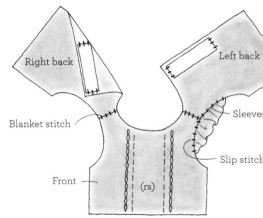

Right back   Left back

Blanket stitch   Sleeve

                              Slip stitch

Front   (rs)

...anket stitch the back pieces to the front along the sides. Embroider the neckline and ...em with a fine blanket stitch. Sew the beads to the front.

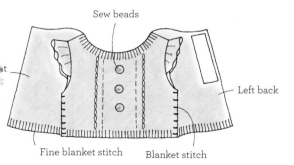

Sew beads

...t

Left back

Fine blanket stitch   Blanket stitch

About 1½" (4 cm) long

3 Striped Tank   Shown on page 48

Materials

White felt: 2" x 4¾" (5 x 12 cm)

...25 embroidery floss in white and blue ...use 1 strand)

...One ¼" x 1" (0.5 x 2.5 cm) piece of hook-...nd-loop tape

...ll-size templates included on page 105.

1. Embroider the front and back following the instructions on the templates.

Front

Embroider two lines for each stripe

...anket stitch the front and back pieces together along the shoulders ...nd sides. Slip stitch the hook-and-loop tape to the back pieces.

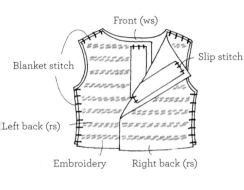

Front (ws)

Blanket stitch

Slip stitch

Left back (rs)

Embroidery   Right back (rs)

About 2" (5 cm) long

44 Maxi Skirt Shown on page 52

Materials

- Blue felt: 3½" x 6" (9 x 15 cm)
- #25 embroidery floss in blue, yellow, orange, and green (use 1 strand)
- One ⅛" (0.3 cm) diameter red bead

Full-size templates included on page 104.

1. Embroider right front following instructions on template. Blanket stitch front and back pieces together at sides. Blanket stitch remaining raw edges. Make buttonhole and attach bead.

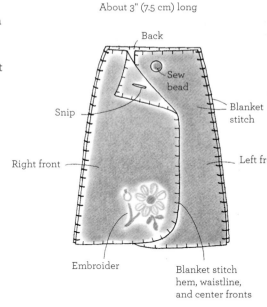

About 3" (7.5 cm) long

Back

Sew bead

Blanket stitch

Snip

Right front

Left fr

Embroider

Blanket stitch hem, waistline, and center fronts

47 Khakis Shown on page 48

Materials

- Khaki felt: 3" x 6" (8 x 15 cm)
- #25 embroidery floss in khaki (use 1 strand)
- One ¼" (0.5 cm) diameter snap

Full-size templates included on page 104.

1. Embroider following instructions on templates. Blanket stitch front and back pieces together at sides and inseam. Sew the snap components to the front pieces.

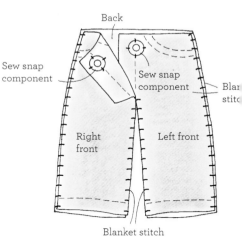

Back

Sew snap component

Sew snap component

Blar stit

Right front

Left front

Blanket stitch

2. Fold the back pleats and slip stitch.

Slip stitch

Back

About 2¾" (7 cm) long

2 Crochet Scarves Shown on page 52

Materials

5 embroidery floss in green
nd blue (use 1 strand)

ols

/1 (2.25 mm) crochet hook

Crochet Pattern

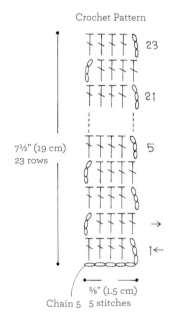

7½" (19 cm)
23 rows

⅝" (1.5 cm)
Chain 5   5 stitches

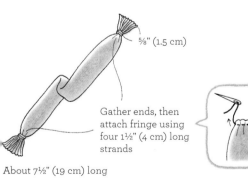

⅝" (1.5 cm)

Gather ends, then
attach fringe using
four 1½" (4 cm) long
strands

About 7½" (19 cm) long

How to Attach Fringe

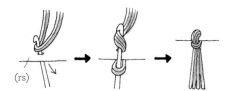

(rs)

54 Capelet Shown on page 50

Materials
- Off-white cotton fabric: 4" x 6" (10 x 15 cm)
- #25 embroidery floss in off-white
  (use 1 strand)
- #5 embroidery floss in off-white
  (use 2 strands)
- 4" (10 cm) of ¹⁄₁₆" (0.2 cm) wide gold cord

Full-size template included on page 109.

1. Before cutting out the capelet, mark the fabric
and fill the outline with cable chain stitch using
#5 embroidery floss.

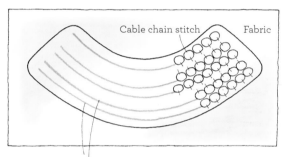

Cable chain stitch   Fabric

Draw light lines using chalk pencil

2. Cut out the capelet. Blanket stitch the edges using
#25 embroidery floss. Thread the cord under the
stitches on the wrong side.

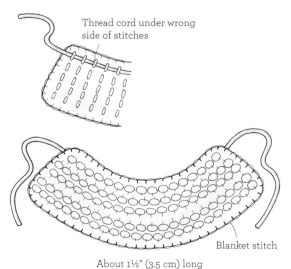

Thread cord under wrong
side of stitches

Blanket stitch

About 1½" (3.5 cm) long

48 Buckle Purse Shown on page 50

Materials

- Red felt: 2½" x 3" (6 x 8 cm)
- Pink felt: 2" x 2½" (5 x 6 cm)
- #25 embroidery floss in red, pink, and silver (use 1 strand)

Full-size templates included on page 107.

1. Blanket stitch the flap to one bag piece. Embroider the tab following instructions on template and slip stitch to the flap.

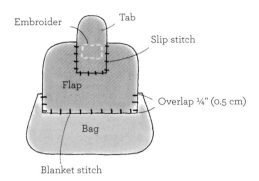

Embroider
Tab
Slip stitch
Flap
Overlap ¼" (0.5 cm)
Bag
Blanket stitch

2. Blanket stitch the two bag pieces together. Insert each end of the handle ¼" (0.5 cm) inside the bag and slip stitch. Sew the snap components to the bag and the flap.

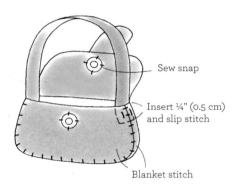

Sew snap
Insert ¼" (0.5 cm) and slip stitch
Blanket stitch

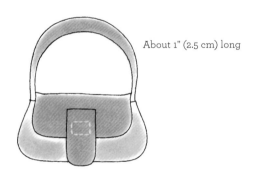

About 1" (2.5 cm) long

56 Wool Mittens Shown on page 52

Materials

- Orange felt: 2½" x 2¾" (6 x 7 cm)
- #25 embroidery floss in orange, light blue, and green (use 1 strand)
- 6" (15 cm) of ¹⁄₁₆" (0.2 cm) thick cord

Full-size templates included on page 103.

* Refer to template for embroidery instructions.

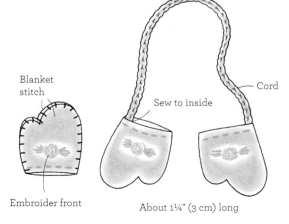

Blanket stitch
Cord
Sew to inside
Embroider front
About 1¼" (3 cm) long

9 Pocket Tote Shown on page 48

Materials

White felt: 2" x 6" (5 x 15 cm)

Navy blue felt: ¾" x 4¾" (2 x 12 cm)

#25 embroidery floss in white (use 1 strand)

Full-size templates included on page 102.

1. Blanket stitch the pocket to one bag piece. Backstitch the handle to the bag piece. Backstitch the remaining handle to the remaining bag piece

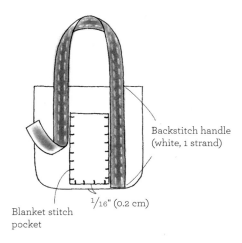

Backstitch handle (white, 1 strand)

Blanket stitch pocket

¹/₁₆" (0.2 cm)

Align two bag pieces and whipstitch together along the bottom.

3. Fold the bag into shape. Insert each gusset and blanket stitch to the bag.

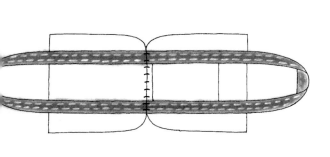

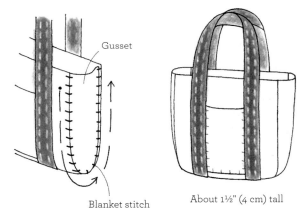

Gusset

Blanket stitch the gusset

About 1½" (4 cm) tall

5 Beaded Necklace Shown on page 53

Materials

One red bead

Two faceted black beads

Four faceted gold beads

Four black beads

Two white beads

Forty silver seed beads

Elastic line

Thread the beads onto the elastic line, then knot.

About 4¼" (11 cm) circumference

White

Black
Gold
Black
Gold
Black
Red   faceted

Collection 4:
Fashionista Friends

Meet our most stylish dolls: Kate and Lisa. They're definitely city girls at heart and are inspired by trendy and happening clothes. They love wearing the latest fashions!

60 + 63 + 68

58 + 65

Meet the Dolls

Kate
Favorite Jewelry: Pearls
Trademark: Long eyelashes

Instructions on page 78

You can change the look of Kate's hair by swapping out her hair accessory.

Look at those long lashes!

Lisa
Favorite Jewelry: Anything that sparkles!
Trademark: Side ponytail

Instructions on page 78

Lisa's side ponytail is made with embroidery floss.

Black leggings go with everything!

This collection is designed and handmade by soeur*2.

Back View

Outfit Ideas

With so many trendy pieces, this wardrobe is fun to mix and match. Here are some chic ideas for dressing Lisa and Kate.

57

Made with a combination of cotton and felt, the Ballet Dress (57) is a complete outfit all by itself!

58 + 64 + 70

The white Halter Top (58), Bow (70), and Chain Strap Purse (64) create a graphic, black and white ensemble.

58 + 63

Match the striped Halter Top (58) with the Tulle Skirt (63) for a simple, bu sophisticated formal outf

59 + 61 + 66 + 69

Throw the Poncho (59) on over the Romper (61) for a fashion-forward look. Add the green Mini Pochette (66) and the purple Rosette (69) for a pop of color.

61 + 70

For a casual, yet classy look, Kate is wearing the Romper (61) and Bow (70). Notice how the leggings peek out at the bottom of the romper!

62 + 66 + 67

Lisa is wearing the Overall Shorts (62) on top of her camisole and leggings. She has tied the Lacy Kerchief (67) around her neck and is carrying a pink Mini Pochette (66).

59 + 61 + 69

Kate is wearing the Poncho (59) and Romper (61) outfit from the opposite page. She has added the purple Rosette (69) to her hair for a splash of color.

Sweet Violet

Kate and Lisa's Wardrobe

Tops and Dress

57
Ballet Dress
Instructions on page 82

Back View

The bow ties
in the back

58
Halter Tops
Instructions on page 83

59
Poncho
Instructions on page 84

60
Tulle Tank
Instructions on page 85

I love getting dressed up. It's fun to put on the Ballet Dress (57), then try it with different hand-bags and hair accessories.

I love all clothes...especially pieces with special details like the ruffles on the side of the Tulle Tank (60)!

Bottoms

61
Romper
Instructions on page 86

Back View

62
Overall Shorts
Instructions on page 84

Use leather
cords for the
suspenders

63
Tulle Skirt
Instructions on page 86

Bags

64
Chain Strap Purse
Instructions on page 87

65
Classic Purse
Instructions on page 87

66
Mini Pochettes
Instructions on page 87

Accessories

68

69

70

67
Lacy Kerchief
Instructions on page 83

68-70
Assorted Hair Accessories
Instructions on page 87

Kate and Lisa
Shown on page 72

Materials (makes 1 doll)

Felt
- Light brown: 5¼" x 6¾" (13 x 17 cm)
- Black: 2" x 2" (5 x 5 cm)

Fabric (for camisole and leggings)
- White cotton: 2" x 2¾" (5 x 6 cm)
- Black cotton: 3⅛" x 3⅛" (8 x 8 cm)

Cutting Instructions
Trace and cut out the full-size templates on page 110. Pin or tape the templates to the felt and cut out following the instructions listed on the templates.

Notions
- #25 embroidery floss in light brown, brown, dark brown, white, black, and pink (use 1 strand)
- Seventeen ⅛" (0.3 cm) diameter pearl beads (for Kate)
- Elastic line (for Kate)
- One ¼" (0.5 cm) diameter snap (for Kate)
- Two small black beads (for Lisa)
- 7" (18 cm) of ¼" (0.7 cm) wide light pink lace (for Lisa)
- About 2½" (6.5 cm) of gold chain (for Lisa)
- One clear rhinestone (for Lisa)
- Two small gold jump rings (for Lisa)
- Stuffing

1. Embroider the hair and face

a. Embroider the front and back hair and the mouth following instructions on the templates.

b. For Kate, embroider the eyes with black embroidery floss. For Lisa, sew the two black beads to the head following placement indicated on the template.

2. Make the head and arms

a. Align the front and back head, then sew together using blanket stitch, inserting the stuffing as you work.

b. Align two arm pieces and sew together using blanket stitch, inserting the stuffing as you work. Repeat for the other arm.

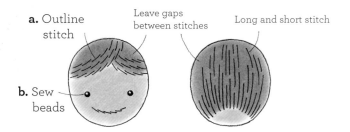

a. Outline stitch

Leave gaps between stitches

Long and short stitch

b. Sew beads

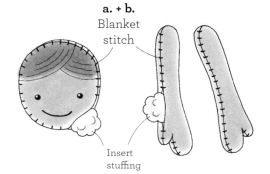

a. + b. Blanket stitch

Insert stuffing

Make the body

Align the leggings and shoe pieces on top of the front and back body pieces. Blanket stitch the front and back together along the legs and toes, inserting stuffing as you work. Make sure to fold the seam allowance under at the hem of the leggings.

Align the camisole pieces on top of the front and back body pieces. Fold the bottom seam allowance under. Blanket stitch the front and back together along the body and sides of the camisole.

For Kate only, embroider the bow on the front camisole using pink embroidery floss.

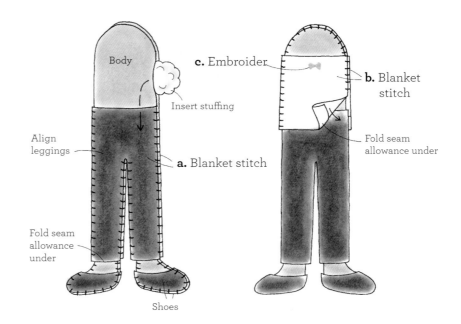

Body

c. Embroider

Insert stuffing

Align leggings

a. Blanket stitch

b. Blanket stitch

Fold seam allowance under

Fold seam allowance under

Shoes

Assemble the dolls

Overlap the head and body ¼" (0.5 cm). Whipstitch the underside of the head to the body.

Sew the arms to the body and knot to secure.

For Lisa only, cut the lace in half. Wrap the lace around the neck and slip stitch to the camisole.

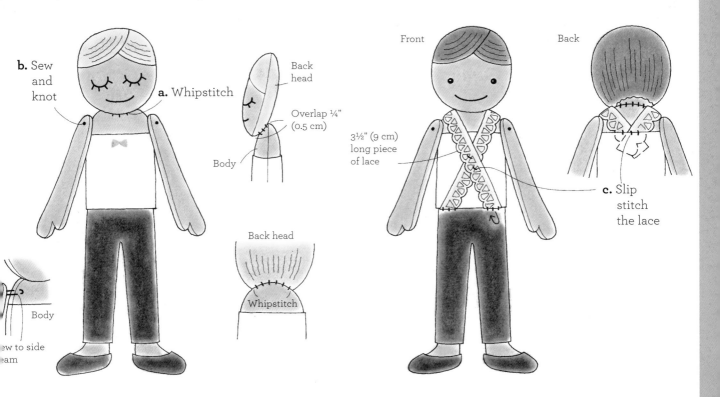

b. Sew and knot

a. Whipstitch

Back head

Overlap ¼" (0.5 cm)

Body

Back head

Whipstitch

Body

Sew to side seam

Front

Back

3½" (9 cm) long piece of lace

c. Slip stitch the lace

5. Make Kate's hair

a. Fold a 39½" (100 cm) long piece of brown embroidery floss in half and knot. Continue folding the floss in half a total of five times.

b. Repeat step **a** using a 27½" (70 cm) long piece of embroidery floss.

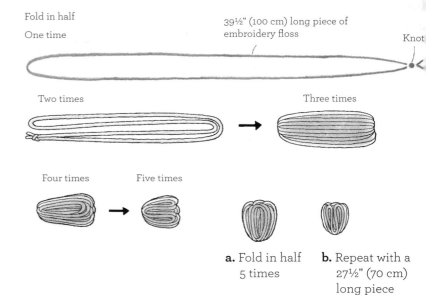

Fold in half
One time

39½" (100 cm) long piece of embroidery floss

Knot

Two times

Three times

Four times

Five times

a. Fold in half 5 times

b. Repeat with a 27½" (70 cm) long piece

6. Finish Kate

a. Overlap the two embroidery floss buns and sew to the head.

b. Sew the female snap component to the front head (this will allow for attaching hair accessories).

c. To make the necklace, thread 15 pearl beads onto a piece of elastic line. Wrap around the neck and knot. Trim the ends and secure with a dab of glue.

d. For the earrings, sew a pearl to each ear.

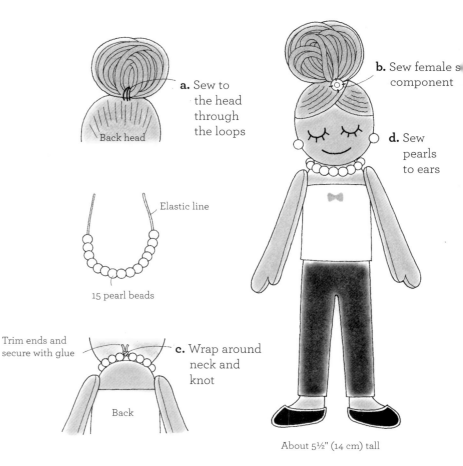

Back head

a. Sew to the head through the loops

b. Sew female s___ component

d. Sew pearls to ears

Elastic line

15 pearl beads

Trim ends and secure with glue

c. Wrap around neck and knot

Back

About 5½" (14 cm) tall

Make Lisa's hair

Fold a 19¾" (50 cm) long piece of dark brown embroidery floss in half and knot. Continue folding the floss in half a total of three times.

Repeat the process used in step **a** to fold a 27½" (70 cm) long piece of embroidery floss in half four times.

Repeat step **b** using a 39½" (100 cm) long piece of embroidery floss.

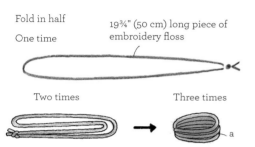

Fold in half
One time

19¾" (50 cm) long piece of embroidery floss

Two times → Three times

a

a

b

c

a. Fold a 19¾" (50 cm) long piece 3 times

b. Fold a 27½" (70 cm) long piece 4 times

c. Fold a 39½" (100 cm) long piece 4 times

Finish Lisa

Overlap the three embroidery floss buns and sew to the head.

To make the necklace, attach a rhinestone to the center of the 1¾" (4.5 cm) long chain using one of the jump rings. Wrap around the neck then attach the other jump ring to connect the ends.

For the earrings, sew a ⅜" (0.8 cm) piece of chain to each ear.

a. Sew to the head through the loops

c. Sew chains
⅜" (0.8 cm)

a

b

c

1¾" (4.5 cm) long chain

b. Attach to the center using jump ring

Rhinestone

Connect using jump ring

About 5½" (14 cm) tall

57 Ballet Dress Shown on page 74

Materials

- White felt: 2" x 4¾" (5 x 12 cm)
- Pink cotton fabric: 2" x 11¾" (5 x 30 cm)
- #25 embroidery floss in black and white (use 1 strand)
- 13¾" (35 cm) of ¼" (0.6 cm) wide black satin ribbon
- One ¼" (0.5 cm) diameter snap

Full-size templates for bodice included on page 111. There is no template for the skirt. Refer to the step 1 diagram for cutting dimensions. Seam allowance is included in the skirt cutting dimensions.

1. Fold each side of the skirt over twice and topstitch. Running stitch along the waistline. Topstitch the bottom hem.

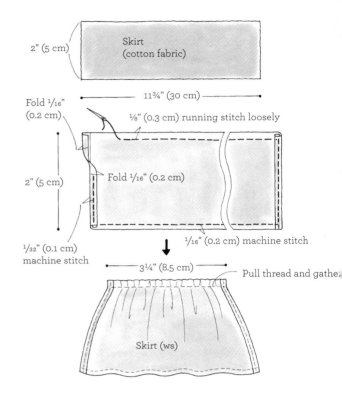

2" (5 cm)

Skirt (cotton fabric)

11¾" (30 cm)

Fold 1/16" (0.2 cm)

⅛" (0.3 cm) running stitch loosely

2" (5 cm)

Fold 1/16" (0.2 cm)

1/32" (0.1 cm) machine stitch

1/16" (0.2 cm) machine stitch

3¼" (8.5 cm)

Pull thread and gather

Skirt (ws)

2. Backstitch the front and back pieces together along the shoulders and sides.

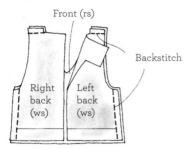

Front (rs)

Backstitch

Right back (ws)

Left back (ws)

3. Align the skirt on top of the bodice and machine sew.

Turn right side out

Align skirt and sew

⅛" (0.3 cm)

Right back

Front (rs)

Left back

Fold sides under ¼" (0.5 cm)

Skirt (rs)

4. Align the ribbon so it is centered at the waist. Running stitch the ribbon to the dress. Sew the snap components to the back of the dress.

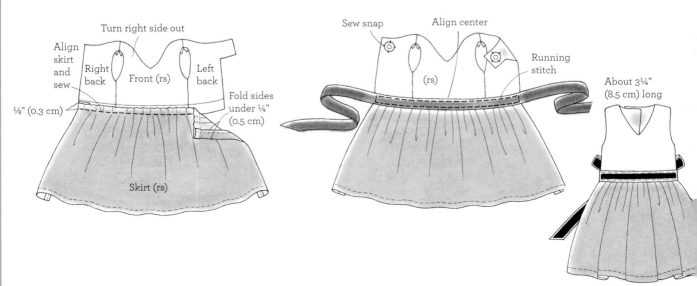

Sew snap

Align center

Running stitch

(rs)

About 3¼" (8.5 cm) long

3 Halter Tops Shown on page 72

Materials

- Gray or black felt: ¾" x ¾" (2 x 2 cm)
- White or black and white striped cotton fabric: 3⅛" x 4" (8 x 10 cm)
- #25 embroidery floss in gray or black (use 1 strand)
- Sewing thread in white
- 2¼" (5.5 cm) of ¼" (0.5 cm) wide light yellow or black satin ribbon
- Two ¼" (0.5 cm) diameter snaps

Full-size templates included on page 111.

1. Fold each side of the top over twice and topstitch. Repeat for top and bottom. Sew a male snap component to the wrong side of the top at **a**.

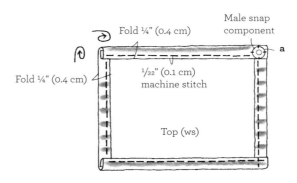

Fold ¼" (0.4 cm)
Male snap component
Fold ¼" (0.4 cm)
1/32" (0.1 cm) machine stitch
a
Top (ws)

Blanket stitch the pocket to the front using embroidery floss. Topstitch the ribbon to the front. Sew the two female snap components to the right side of the top at **a** and **b** and the remaining male snap component to the wrong side of the ribbon at **b**. Close the snaps to form the halter top into shape.

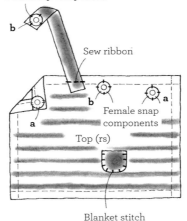

Male snap component
b
Sew ribbon
b
a
Female snap components
a
Top (rs)
Blanket stitch

About 2½" (6 cm) long
Snap **a** to **a** and **b** to **b**

7 Lacy Kerchief Shown on page 75

Materials

- 1½" x 3½" (4 x 9 cm) of white lace
- 4¾" (12 cm) of 1/16" (0.2 cm) wide pink satin ribbon
- #25 embroidery floss in white (use 1 strand)

There is no template for this project.

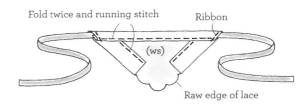

Fold twice and running stitch
Ribbon
(ws)
Raw edge of lace

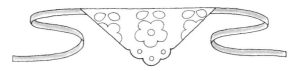

About 3" (7.5 cm) wide

59 Poncho Shown on page 74

Materials

- Striped cotton fabric: 5¼" x 5¼" (13 x 13 cm)
- #25 embroidery floss in black (use 2 strands)
- Sewing thread in white
- One ¼" (0.5 cm) diameter snap

Full-size template included on page 111.

1. Fold each straight raw edge over twice and topstitch. Topstitch along the outer curved edge without folding. Blanket stitch along the neckline curve.

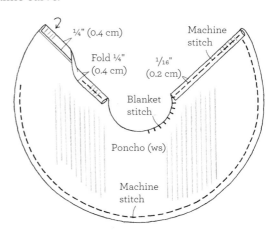

¼" (0.4 cm)

Machine stitch

Fold ¼" (0.4 cm)

¹/₁₆" (0.2 cm)

Blanket stitch

Poncho (ws)

Machine stitch

2. Fold the poncho into shape along the fold lines. Sew the tacks through the multiple layers of fabric as shown in the diagram below to create sleeves. Sew the snap components to the poncho.

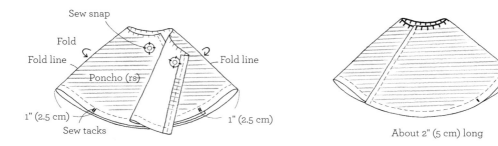

Sew snap

Fold

Fold line

Fold line

Poncho (rs)

1" (2.5 cm)

Sew tacks

1" (2.5 cm)

About 2" (5 cm) long

62 Overall Shorts Shown on page 75

Materials

- Light gray felt: 2" x 6" (5 x 15 cm)
- #25 embroidery floss in gray (use 1 strand)
- 7" (18 cm) of ⅛" (0.3 cm) wide flat leather cord
- One ¼" (0.5 cm) diameter snap

Full-size templates included on page 110.

1. With right sides together, backstitch the front and back pieces together along the sides and inseam.

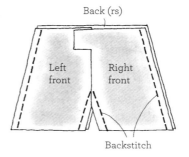

Back (rs)

Left front

Right front

Backstitch

urn right side out. Sew the snap
omponents to the front pieces.

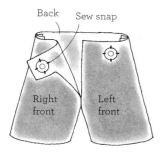

Back   Sew snap

Right front

Left front

3. Cut the leather cord in half. Sew one end of each cord to the front and the other to the back, crossing the cords.

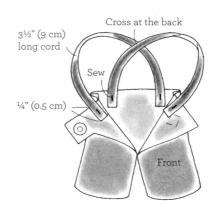

Cross at the back

3½" (9 cm) long cord

Sew

¼" (0.5 cm)

Front

About 1½" (4 cm) long

Tulle Tank   Shown on page 72

aterials

.ight blue felt: 2¾" x 4¾"
7 x 12 cm)

25 embroidery floss in
.ght blue (use 1 strand)

" x 2" (5 x 5 cm) of
.lack tulle

One ¼" (0.5 cm)
.iameter snap

l-size templates included
page 112.

1. With right sides together, backstitch the front and back pieces together along the shoulders and sides.

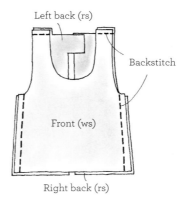

Left back (rs)

Backstitch

Front (ws)

Right back (rs)

urn the top right side out. Make eight tufts of
.lle. Sew four tufts to each side of the top.

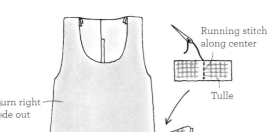

Running stitch along center

Tulle

urn right
.de out

Gather and sew

3. Sew the snap components to the back of the top.

Sew snaps

Left back (rs)

Right back (rs)

About 2¼" (5.5 cm) long

61 Romper Shown on page 74

Materials

- Heather gray felt: 4¼" x 6" (11 x 15 cm)
- #25 embroidery floss in gray (use 1 strand)
- One ¼" (0.5 cm) diameter snap

Full-size templates included on page 112.

1. Backstitch the front and back pieces together along the shoulders, sides, and inseam.

2. Turn right side out and whipstitch the cent[er] back edges together as indicated on templ[ate]. Sew the snap components to the back piec[e]

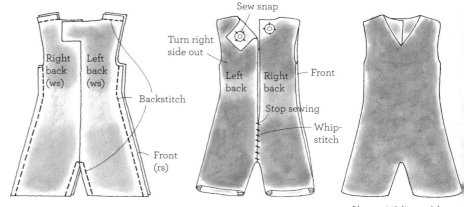

Right back (ws) Left back (ws) Backstitch Front (rs)

Sew snap Turn right side out Left back Right back Front Stop sewing Whip-stitch

About 3¼" (8.5 cm) long

63 Tulle Skirt Shown on page 72

Materials

- 2" x 13¾" (5 x 35 cm) of black tulle
- Black hand sewing thread
- 12¾" (32 cm) of ¼" (0.6 cm) wide black satin ribbon

There is no template for this project. Refer to the step 1 diagram for cutting dimensions. Seam allowance is included in the skirt cutting dimensions.

1. Fold top edge over and running stitch to create a waistband.

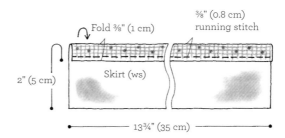

Fold ⅜" (1 cm) ⅜" (0.8 cm) running stitch 2" (5 cm) Skirt (ws) 13¾" (35 cm)

2. Insert ribbon through waistband. Gather the skirt to 3⅛" (8 cm). Sew to secure ribbon in place.

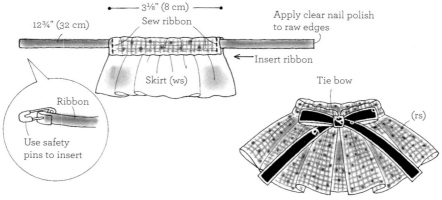

12¾" (32 cm) 3⅛" (8 cm) Sew ribbon Apply clear nail polish to raw edges Insert ribbon Skirt (ws) Ribbon Use safety pins to insert Tie bow (rs)

About 1½" (4 cm) long

4 Chain Strap Purse, 65 Classic Purse, & 66 Mini Pochettes

own on pages 72 and 74

aterials

r All

elt: 1¼" x 2" (3 x 5 cm) of black, red,
reen, or dark pink

25 embroidery floss in same color
s felt (use 1 strand)

ne gold seed bead

r Chain Strap Purse

" (10 cm) of gold chain

r Classic Purse

" (10 cm) of ⅛" (0.3 cm) wide
white satin ribbon

r Mini Pochette

½" (4 cm) of gold chain

l-size templates included on page 112.

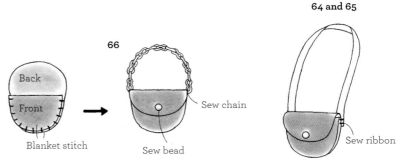

66

Back

Front

Blanket stitch

Sew chain

Sew bead

64 and 65

Sew ribbon

About ¾" (2 cm) wide

3-70 Assorted Hair Accessories

Shown on pages 72-74

aterials

r Hair Ribbon #68

" (15 cm) of ¼" (0.5 cm) wide black
atin ribbon

25 embroidery floss in black
use 1 strand)

ne ¼" (0.5 cm) diameter snap

r Rosette #69

ne ⅝" (1.5 cm) diameter purple rosette

25 embroidery floss in purple
use 1 strand)

ne ¼" (0.5 cm) diameter snap

r Bow #70

elt: ¾" x 4¼" (2 x 11 cm) of white
r light blue

25 embroidery floss in white or light
lue (use 1 strand)

ne ¼" (0.5 cm) diameter snap

ere is no template for this project.

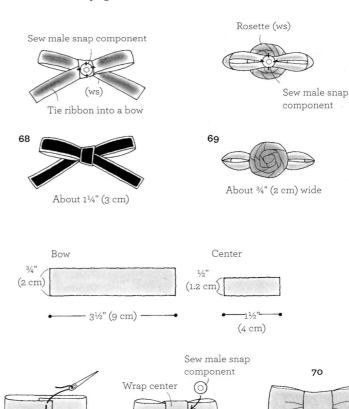

Sew male snap component

(ws)

Tie ribbon into a bow

Rosette (ws)

Sew male snap
component

68

About 1¼" (3 cm)

69

About ¾" (2 cm) wide

Bow

¾"
(2 cm)

3½" (9 cm)

Center

½"
(1.2 cm)

1½"
(4 cm)

Sew short ends of bow
and pull to gather

Wrap center

Sew male snap
component

Slip stitch

70

About 1½" (4 cm) wide

Doll Making Guide

The dolls and clothes in this book are quick and easy to make. The following guide covers the entire construction process from cutting and sewing to embroidering the finishing touches.

Tools & Materials

All of the projects in this book are made with everyday craft materials, so you may already have everything you need to get started. Here is a list of the basic tools and materials you will need to complete the various projects:

Tools
- Pencil or marker
- Ruler
- Tape
- Scissors
- Embroidery needle
- Tapestry needle
- Crochet hook

Materials
- Felt
- Fabric
- #25 embroidery floss
- Beads and buttons
- Yarn, leather cord, lace, ribbon, rickrack, and tulle
- Elastic tape

Transferring the Templates & Cutting

Felt doesn't have a right or wrong side. Choose one side as the wrong side and place the template on that side. Mark the outline while holding the template steady with your hand. You can also tape the template to the felt.

Use either a chalk pencil, colored pencil, or fabric marker to mark the felt. For dark colored felt, use a white or yellow pencil so you can see the lines clearly.

Using a ruler, copy the seam allowance line from the template and mark it on the felt or fabric. Cut each piece out along the outline.

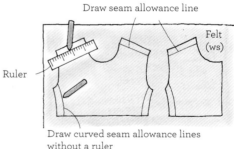

Draw seam allowance line

Felt (ws)

Ruler

Draw curved seam allowance lines without a ruler

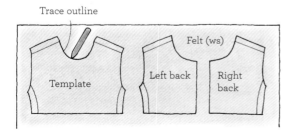

Trace outline

Template

Felt (ws)

Left back

Right back

Cut along outline

wing

n felt and fabric are used in this book. Unless otherwise
ed, always use thread in a coordinating color to your
erial. Use #25 embroidery floss for sewing felt and
hine sewing thread for sewing fabric. The raw edges
elt do not need to be finished since this material won't
l. To finish raw fabric edges, zigzag stitch if machine
ing, or fold the raw edge over twice and slip stitch
and.

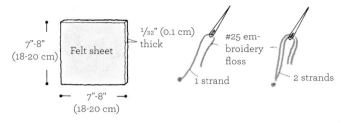

u try sewing two sheets of felt together by stacking them, the felt won't stay aligned because it is so thick. To keep
sheets aligned while you sew, insert the needle into the felt vertically, then bring the needle back through the starting
t. Tighten each stitch as you sew. It's better to hold the felt in position with your fingers rather than using pins. The
wing guide illustrates different techniques for sewing felt together.

kstitch

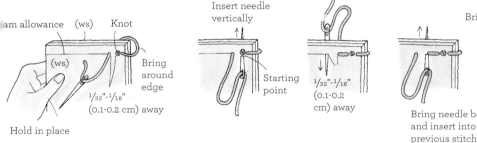

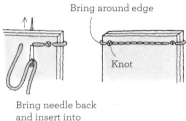

nket Stitch

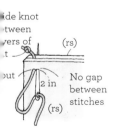

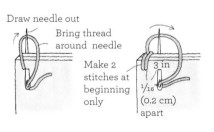

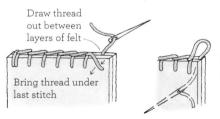

Running Stitch

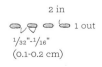

Slip Stitch

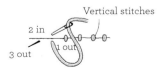

Embroidery Stitch Guide

Outline Stitch

Backstitch

Scoop 2 stitches worth of fabric at a time

Running Stitch

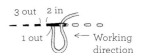

French Knot

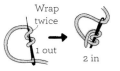

Straight Stitch

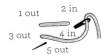

Satin Stitch

Bullion Stitch

Wrap thread around needle several times

Pull thread taut and insert needle

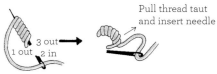

Lazy Daisy Stitch

Bring thread under needle

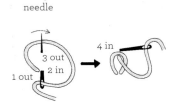

Cable Stitch

Scoop thread   Scoop again   Scoop

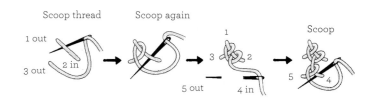

Full-Size Templates

na and Anya
e 16

Straight stitch
(cream, 2 strands)

French knot
(Irina: dark brown, 2 strands
Anya: light blue, 2 strands)

Backstitch
(red, 2 strands)

Red felt

Position to attach arms

Right arm
(cut 2 of cream felt)

Body (cut 2 of cream felt)

Left arm
(cut 2 of cream felt)

Front hair (cut 1 of dark brown felt for Irina and 1 of yellow felt for Anya)

Back hair (cut 1 of dark brown felt for Irina and 1 of yellow felt for Anya)

Position to attach braids or buns

Seam allowance

Right leg
(cut 2 of light brown felt for Irina and 2 of maroon felt for Anya)

Seam allowance

Left leg
(cut 2 of light brown felt for Irina and 2 of maroon felt for Anya)

Button
(front only)

Camisole
(cut 2 of light blue felt for Irina and 2 of light pink felt for Anya)

a's shoe strap
2 of black felt)

Running stitch
(dark brown, 2 strands)

Anya's right shoe
(cut 2 of black felt)

Anya's left shoe
(cut 2 of black felt)

Seam allowance

Right pants
(cut 2 of light blue felt for Irina and 2 of light pink felt for Anya)

Seam allowance

Left pants
(cut 2 of light blue felt for Irina and 2 of light pink felt for Anya)

5 Vintage Vest Page 23

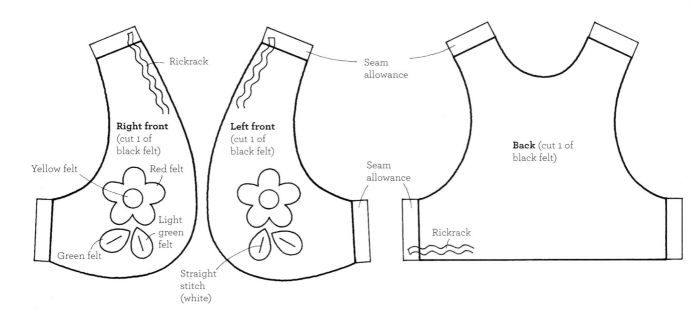

Right front (cut 1 of black felt)

Rickrack

Yellow felt

Red felt

Light green felt

Green felt

Straight stitch (white)

Left front (cut 1 of black felt)

Seam allowance

Seam allowance

Back (cut 1 of black felt)

Rickrack

13 Matryoshka Bag Page 30

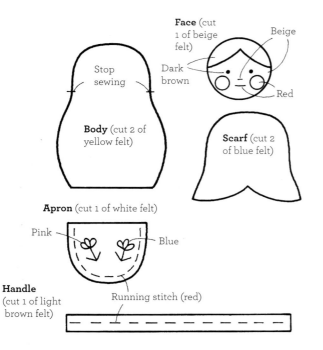

Face (cut 1 of beige felt)

Beige

Dark brown

Red

Stop sewing

Body (cut 2 of yellow felt)

Scarf (cut 2 of blue felt)

Apron (cut 1 of white felt)

Pink

Blue

Handle (cut 1 of light brown felt)

Running stitch (red)

Embroidery Guide for Matryoshka Bag
- Use 1 strand of embroidery floss for the mouth and 2 strands for all other embroidery.
- Lazy daisy stitch: Flowers
- Straight stitch: Stem, leaf, mouth, and nose
- French knot stitch: Eyes

14 Flower Tote Page 29

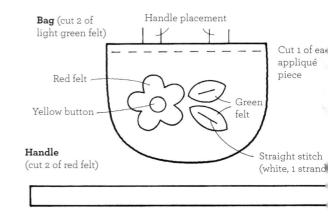

Bag (cut 2 of light green felt)

Handle placement

Cut 1 of ea appliqué piece

Red felt

Yellow button

Green felt

Handle (cut 2 of red felt)

Straight stitch (white, 1 strand

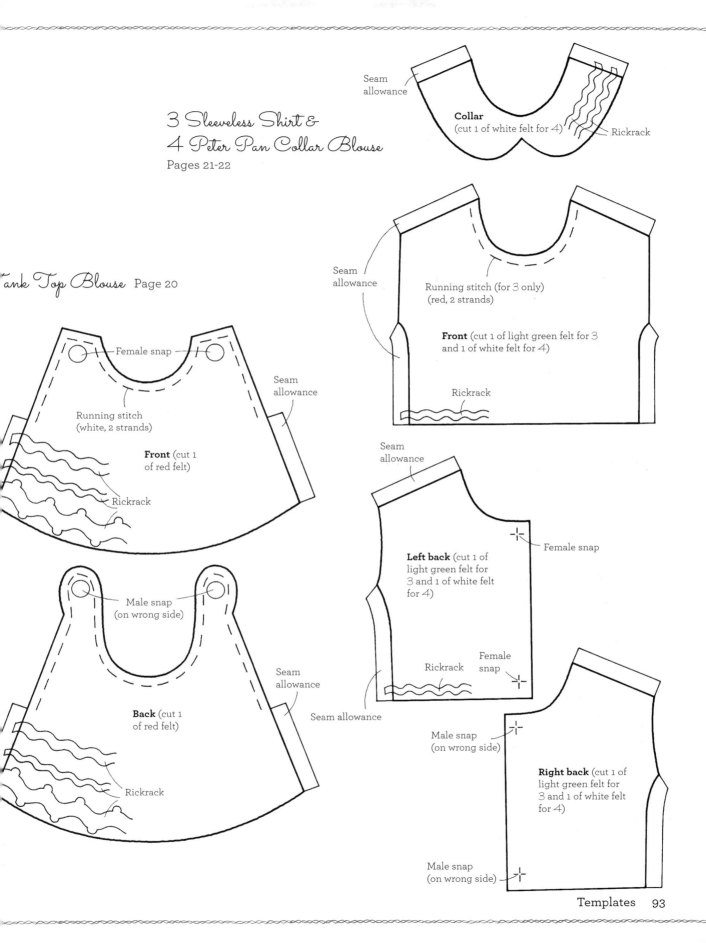

3 Sleeveless Shirt &
4 Peter Pan Collar Blouse
Pages 21-22

Seam allowance

Collar
(cut 1 of white felt for 4)

Rickrack

Tank Top Blouse Page 20

Seam allowance

Running stitch (for 3 only)
(red, 2 strands)

Front (cut 1 of light green felt for 3
and 1 of white felt for 4)

Rickrack

Female snap

Running stitch
(white, 2 strands)

Front (cut 1
of red felt)

Rickrack

Seam allowance

Seam allowance

Male snap
(on wrong side)

Left back (cut 1 of
light green felt for
3 and 1 of white felt
for 4)

Female snap

Rickrack

Female snap

Seam allowance

Seam allowance

Back (cut 1
of red felt)

Rickrack

Male snap
(on wrong side)

Right back (cut 1 of
light green felt for
3 and 1 of white felt
for 4)

Male snap
(on wrong side)

12 Blue Jeans Page 29

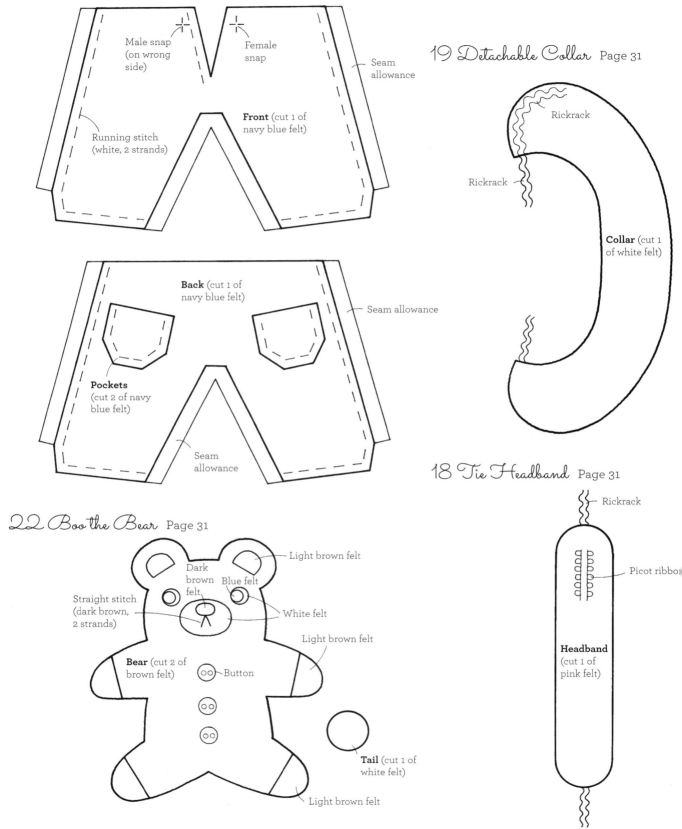

Male snap (on wrong side)

Female snap

Seam allowance

Front (cut 1 of navy blue felt)

Running stitch (white, 2 strands)

Back (cut 1 of navy blue felt)

Seam allowance

Pockets (cut 2 of navy blue felt)

Seam allowance

22 Boo the Bear Page 31

Light brown felt

Dark brown felt

Blue felt

Straight stitch (dark brown, 2 strands)

White felt

Light brown felt

Bear (cut 2 of brown felt)

Button

Tail (cut 1 of white felt)

Light brown felt

19 Detachable Collar Page 31

Rickrack

Rickrack

Collar (cut 1 of white felt)

18 Tie Headband Page 31

Rickrack

Picot ribbon

Headband (cut 1 of pink felt)

10 *Linen Slacks* Page 28

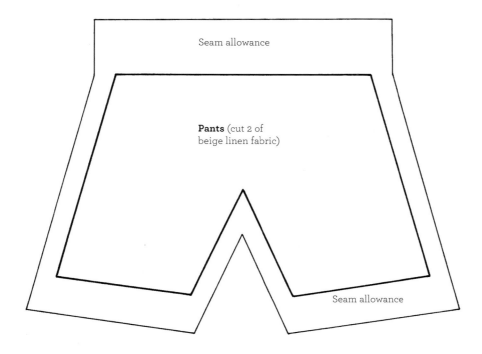

Seam allowance

Pants (cut 2 of beige linen fabric)

Seam allowance

11 *Gingham Pants* Page 28

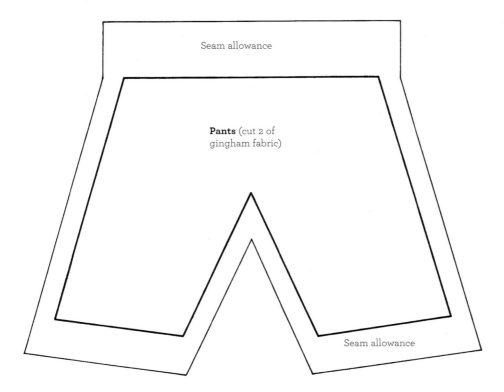

Seam allowance

Pants (cut 2 of gingham fabric)

Seam allowance

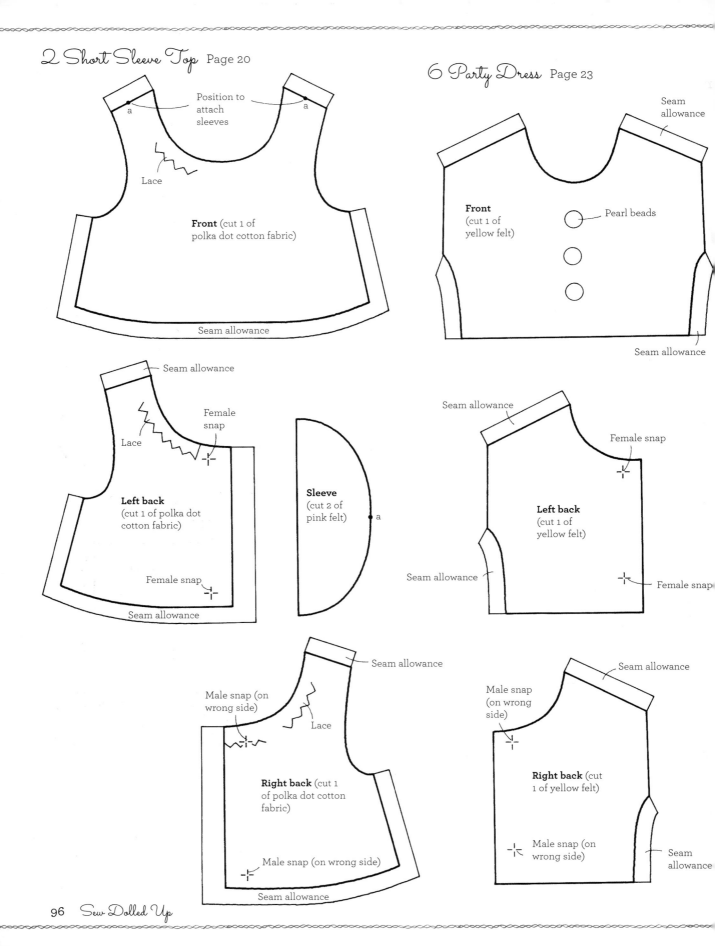

2 Short Sleeve Top Page 20

Position to attach sleeves

a   a

Lace

Front (cut 1 of polka dot cotton fabric)

Seam allowance

Seam allowance

Lace

Female snap

Left back
(cut 1 of polka dot cotton fabric)

Female snap

Seam allowance

Sleeve
(cut 2 of pink felt)

a

Seam allowance

Male snap (on wrong side)

Lace

Right back (cut 1 of polka dot cotton fabric)

Male snap (on wrong side)

Seam allowance

6 Party Dress Page 23

Seam allowance

Front
(cut 1 of yellow felt)

Pearl beads

Seam allowance

Seam allowance

Female snap

Left back
(cut 1 of yellow felt)

Seam allowance

Female snap

Seam allowance

Male snap
(on wrong side)

Right back (cut 1 of yellow felt)

Male snap (on wrong side)

Seam allowance

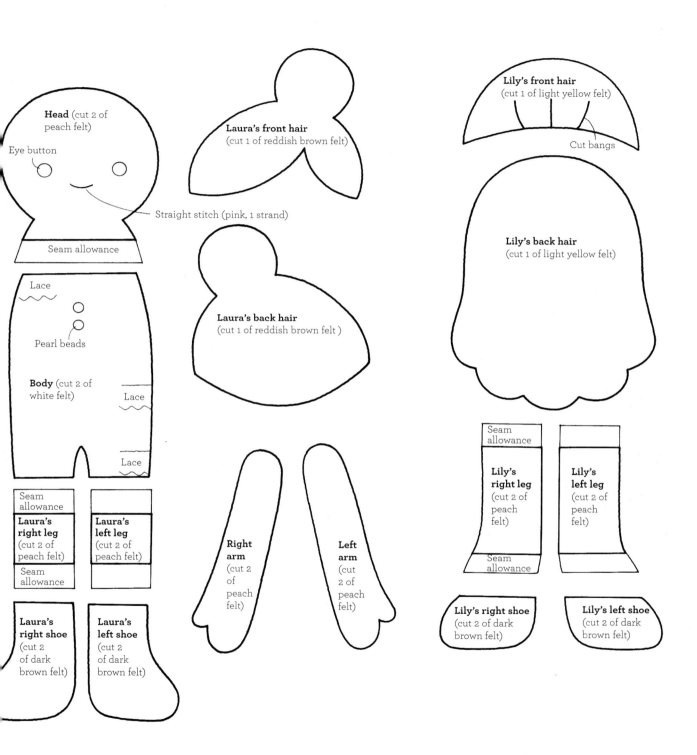

Head (cut 2 of peach felt)

Eye button

Straight stitch (pink, 1 strand)

Seam allowance

Lace

Pearl beads

Body (cut 2 of white felt)

Lace

Lace

Seam allowance

Laura's right leg (cut 2 of peach felt)

Seam allowance

Laura's left leg (cut 2 of peach felt)

Laura's right shoe (cut 2 of dark brown felt)

Laura's left shoe (cut 2 of dark brown felt)

Laura's front hair (cut 1 of reddish brown felt)

Laura's back hair (cut 1 of reddish brown felt)

Right arm (cut 2 of peach felt)

Left arm (cut 2 of peach felt)

Lily's front hair (cut 1 of light yellow felt)

Cut bangs

Lily's back hair (cut 1 of light yellow felt)

Seam allowance

Lily's right leg (cut 2 of peach felt)

Lily's left leg (cut 2 of peach felt)

Seam allowance

Lily's right shoe (cut 2 of dark brown felt)

Lily's left shoe (cut 2 of dark brown felt)

25 Shift Dress Page 43

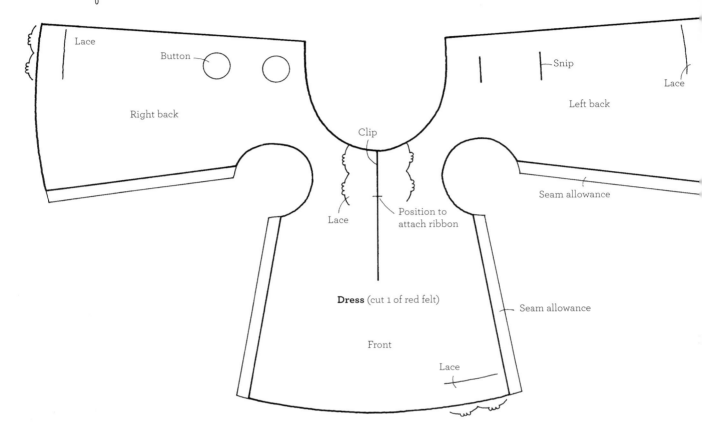

Lace

Button

Right back

Snip

Lace

Left back

Clip

Seam allowance

Lace

Position to attach ribbon

Dress (cut 1 of red felt)

Seam allowance

Front

Lace

30 Wrap Skirt Page 46

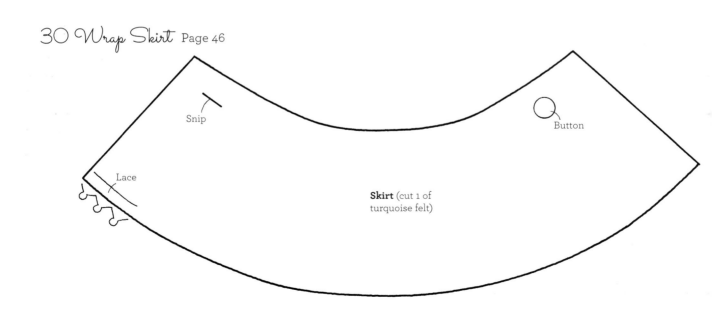

Snip

Button

Lace

Skirt (cut 1 of turquoise felt)

Pleated Skirt Page 45

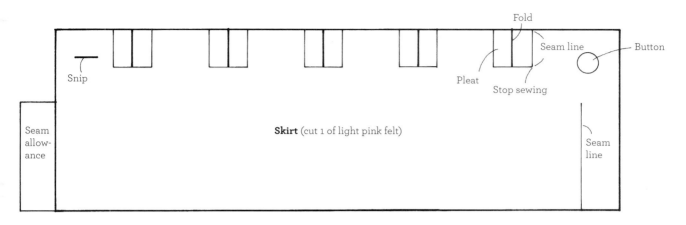

Fold

Seam line

Button

Snip

Pleat

Stop sewing

Seam allowance

Skirt (cut 1 of light pink felt)

Seam line

Sundress Page 43

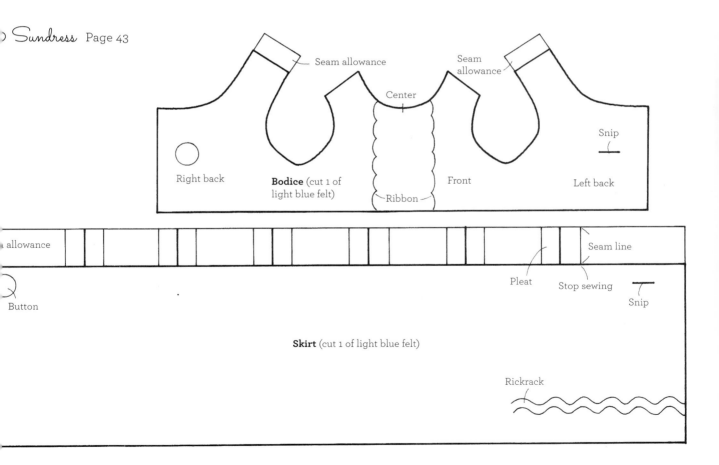

Seam allowance

Seam allowance

Center

Snip

Right back

Bodice (cut 1 of light blue felt)

Ribbon

Front

Left back

allowance

Seam line

Pleat

Stop sewing

Snip

Button

Skirt (cut 1 of light blue felt)

Rickrack

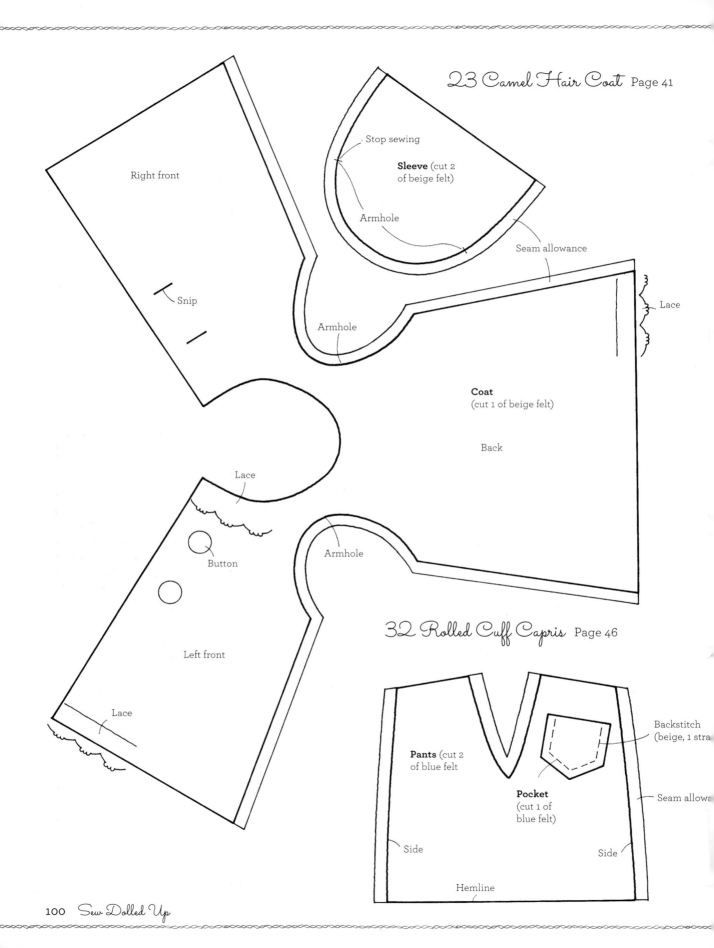

Right front

Snip

Sleeve (cut 2 of beige felt)

Stop sewing

Armhole

Armhole

Seam allowance

Lace

Coat
(cut 1 of beige felt)

Back

Lace

Button

Armhole

Left front

Lace

Backstitch
(beige, 1 stra

Pants (cut 2
of blue felt

Pocket
(cut 1 of
blue felt)

Seam allowa

Side

Side

Hemline

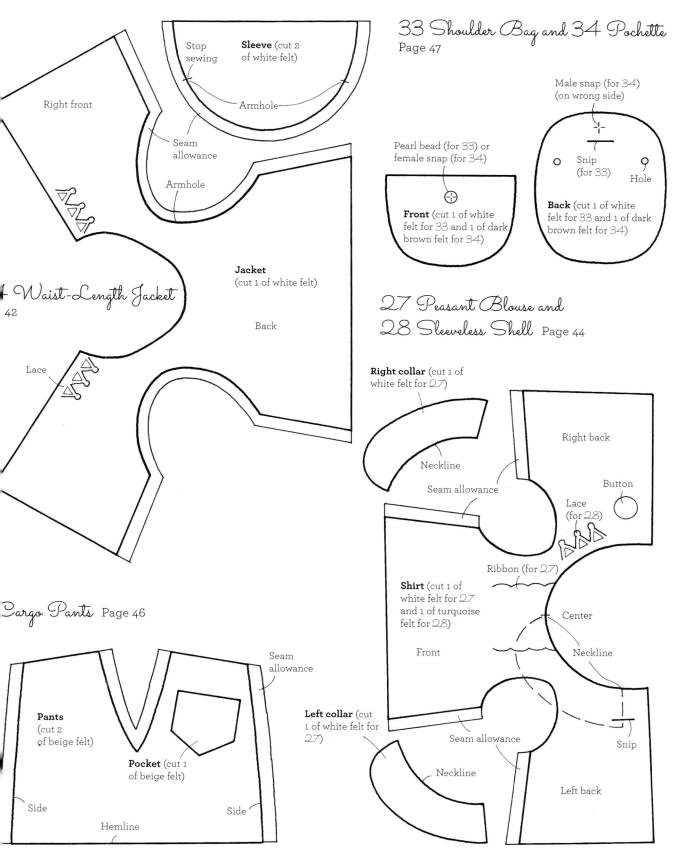

Sleeve (cut 2 of white felt)

Stop sewing

Armhole

Seam allowance

Armhole

33 Shoulder Bag and 34 Pochette
Page 47

Male snap (for 34) (on wrong side)

Pearl bead (for 33) or female snap (for 34)

Snip (for 33)

Hole

Front (cut 1 of white felt for 33 and 1 of dark brown felt for 34)

Back (cut 1 of white felt for 33 and 1 of dark brown felt for 34)

Right front

Jacket (cut 1 of white felt)

Back

Waist-Length Jacket
42

Lace

27 Peasant Blouse and 28 Sleeveless Shell Page 44

Right collar (cut 1 of white felt for 27)

Neckline

Seam allowance

Right back

Button

Lace (for 28)

Ribbon (for 27)

Shirt (cut 1 of white felt for 27 and 1 of turquoise felt for 28)

Front

Center

Neckline

Cargo Pants Page 46

Seam allowance

Pants (cut 2 of beige felt)

Pocket (cut 1 of beige felt)

Left collar (cut 1 of white felt for 27)

Seam allowance

Neckline

Left back

Snip

Side

Side

Hemline

Lydia and Amelia
Page 56

49 Pocket Tote
Page 71

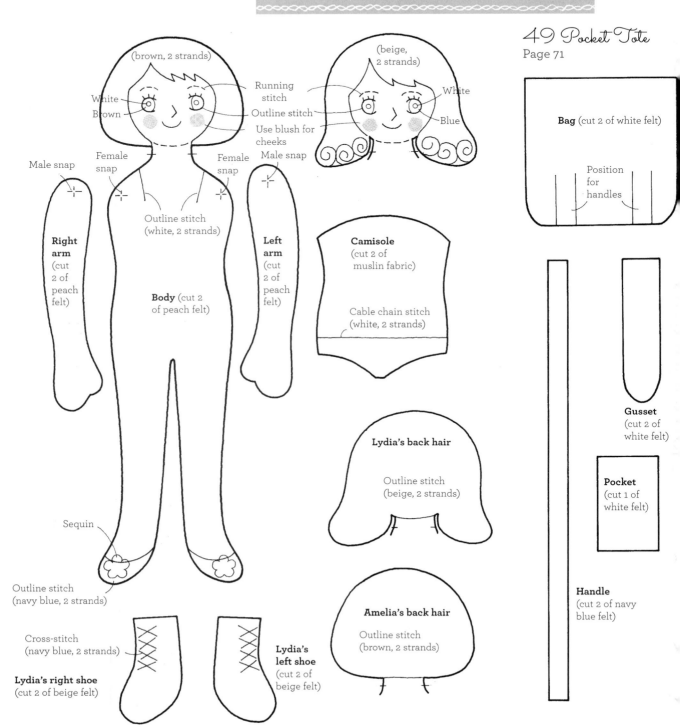

(brown, 2 strands)

(beige, 2 strands)

White
Brown

Running stitch
Outline stitch
Use blush for cheeks

White
Blue

Male snap

Female snap

Female snap

Male snap

Right arm (cut 2 of peach felt)

Outline stitch (white, 2 strands)

Body (cut 2 of peach felt)

Left arm (cut 2 of peach felt)

Camisole (cut 2 of muslin fabric)

Cable chain stitch (white, 2 strands)

Bag (cut 2 of white felt)

Position for handles

Gusset (cut 2 of white felt)

Lydia's back hair

Outline stitch (beige, 2 strands)

Pocket (cut 1 of white felt)

Sequin

Outline stitch (navy blue, 2 strands)

Cross-stitch (navy blue, 2 strands)

Lydia's right shoe (cut 2 of beige felt)

Lydia's left shoe (cut 2 of beige felt)

Amelia's back hair

Outline stitch (brown, 2 strands)

Handle (cut 2 of navy blue felt)

Argyle Shell Page 65

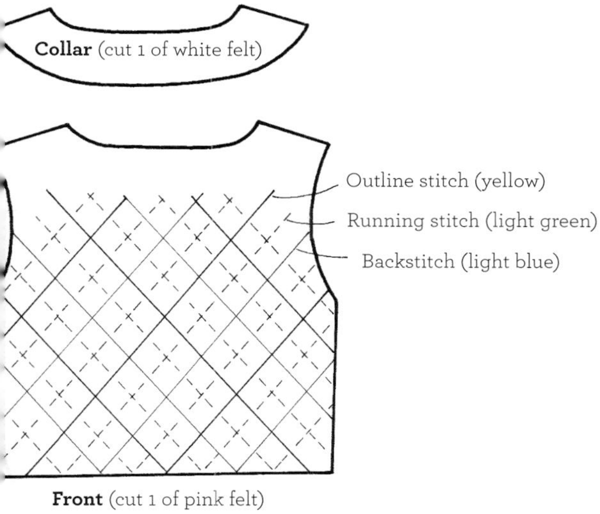

Collar (cut 1 of white felt)

Outline stitch (yellow)

Running stitch (light green)

Backstitch (light blue)

Front (cut 1 of pink felt)

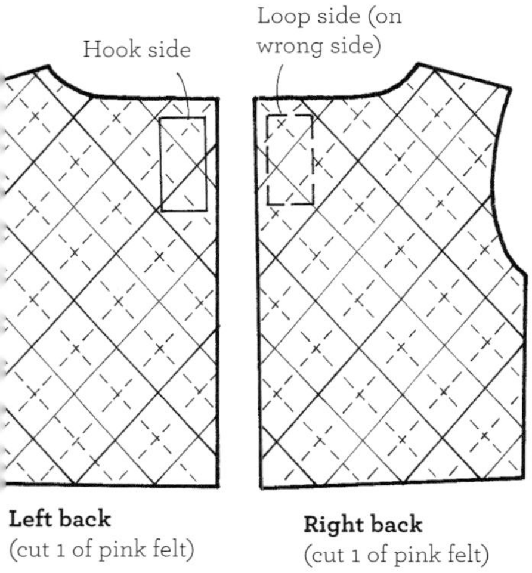

Hook side

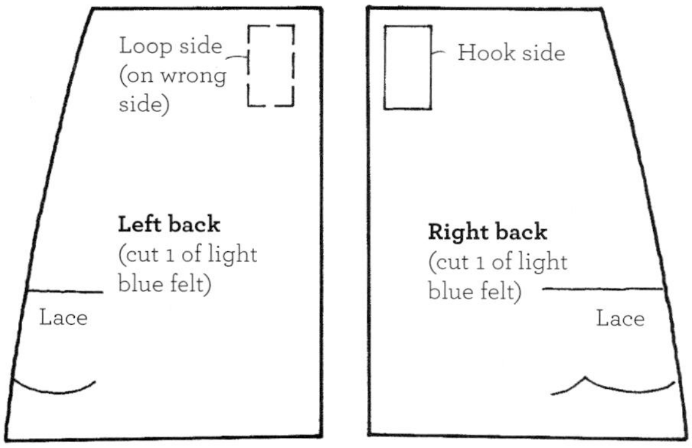

Loop side (on wrong side)

Left back
(cut 1 of pink felt)

Right back
(cut 1 of pink felt)

Cloche Page 59

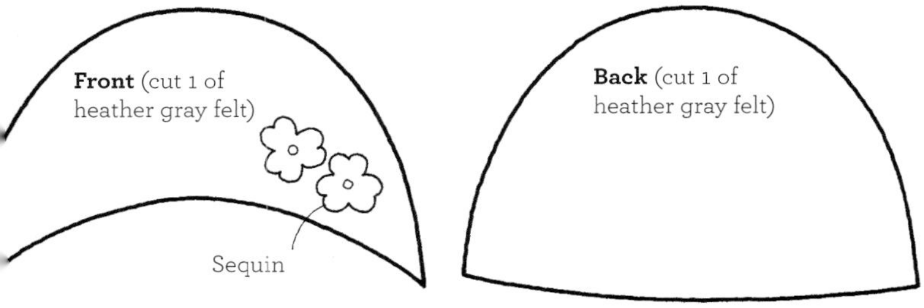

Front (cut 1 of heather gray felt)

Back (cut 1 of heather gray felt)

Sequin

45 Lace Skirt Page 61

Loop side (on wrong side)

Hook side

Left back
(cut 1 of light blue felt)

Lace

Right back
(cut 1 of light blue felt)

Lace

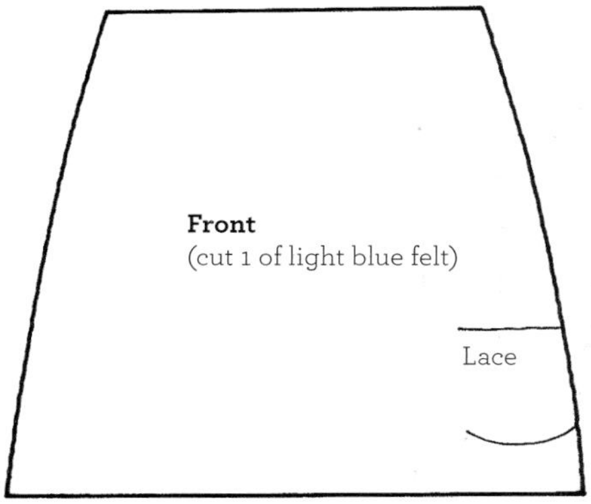

Front
(cut 1 of light blue felt)

Lace

56 Wool Mittens Page 70

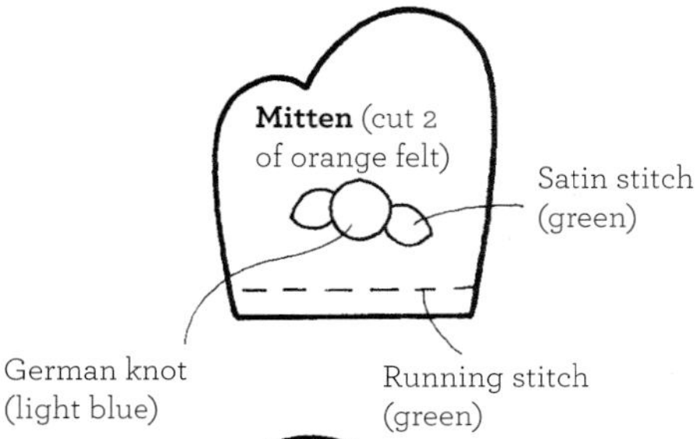

Mitten (cut 2 of orange felt)

Satin stitch (green)

German knot (light blue)

Running stitch (green)

Mitten (cut 2 of orange felt)

44 Maxi Skirt Page 68

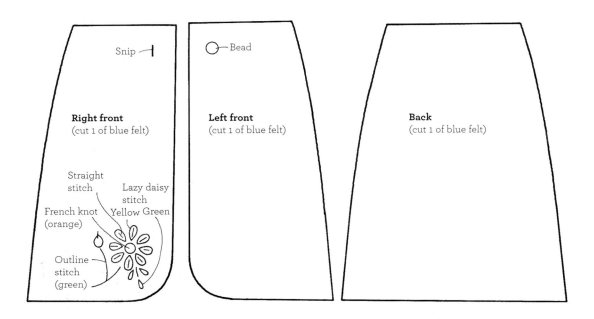

Snip

Right front
(cut 1 of blue felt)

Straight stitch

French knot (orange)

Lazy daisy stitch Yellow Green

Outline stitch (green)

Bead

Left front
(cut 1 of blue felt)

Back
(cut 1 of blue felt)

47 Khakis Page 68

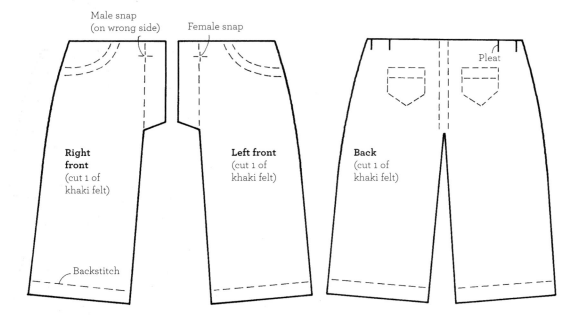

Male snap (on wrong side)

Female snap

Right front
(cut 1 of khaki felt)

Left front
(cut 1 of khaki felt)

Back
(cut 1 of khaki felt)

Pleat

Backstitch

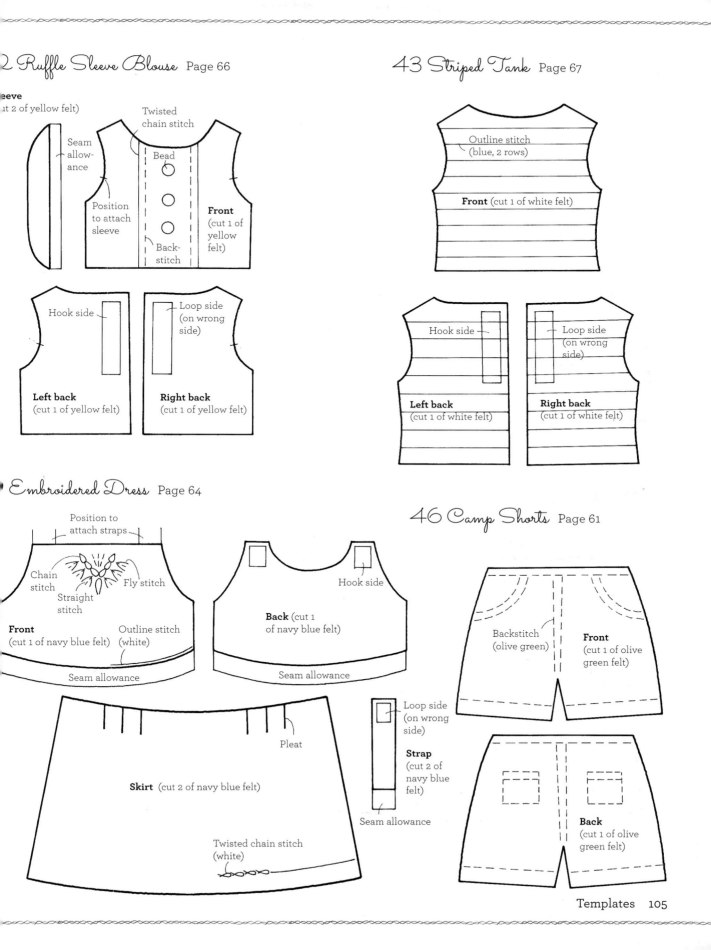

42 Ruffle Sleeve Blouse Page 66

Sleeve
(cut 2 of yellow felt)

Seam allowance

Twisted chain stitch

Bead

Position to attach sleeve

Backstitch

Front (cut 1 of yellow felt)

Hook side

Loop side (on wrong side)

Left back (cut 1 of yellow felt)

Right back (cut 1 of yellow felt)

43 Striped Tank Page 67

Outline stitch (blue, 2 rows)

Front (cut 1 of white felt)

Hook side

Loop side (on wrong side)

Left back (cut 1 of white felt)

Right back (cut 1 of white felt)

Embroidered Dress Page 64

Position to attach straps

Chain stitch

Fly stitch

Straight stitch

Front (cut 1 of navy blue felt)

Outline stitch (white)

Seam allowance

Hook side

Back (cut 1 of navy blue felt)

Seam allowance

Skirt (cut 2 of navy blue felt)

Pleat

Loop side (on wrong side)

Strap (cut 2 of navy blue felt)

Seam allowance

Twisted chain stitch (white)

46 Camp Shorts Page 61

Backstitch (olive green)

Front (cut 1 of olive green felt)

Back (cut 1 of olive green felt)

38 Collarless Jacket Page 63

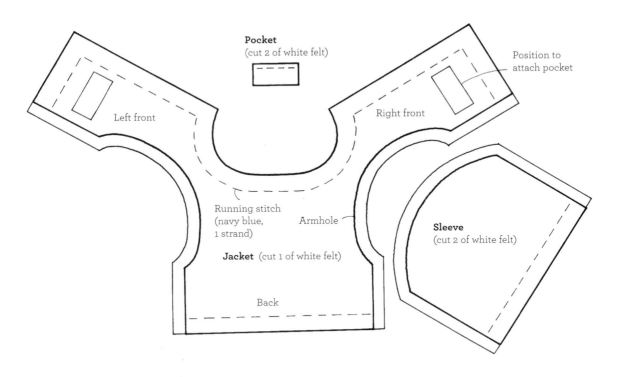

Pocket
(cut 2 of white felt)

Position to attach pocket

Left front

Right front

Running stitch
(navy blue,
1 strand)

Armhole

Sleeve
(cut 2 of white felt)

Jacket (cut 1 of white felt)

Back

37 Camel Blazer Page 62

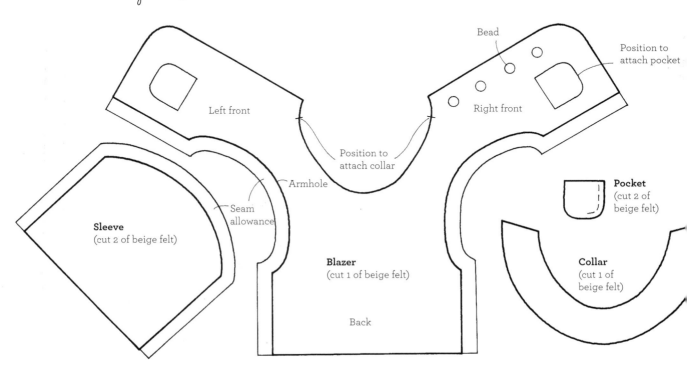

Bead

Position to attach pocket

Left front

Right front

Position to attach collar

Armhole

Seam allowance

Sleeve
(cut 2 of beige felt)

Pocket
(cut 2 of beige felt)

Blazer
(cut 1 of beige felt)

Collar
(cut 1 of beige felt)

Back

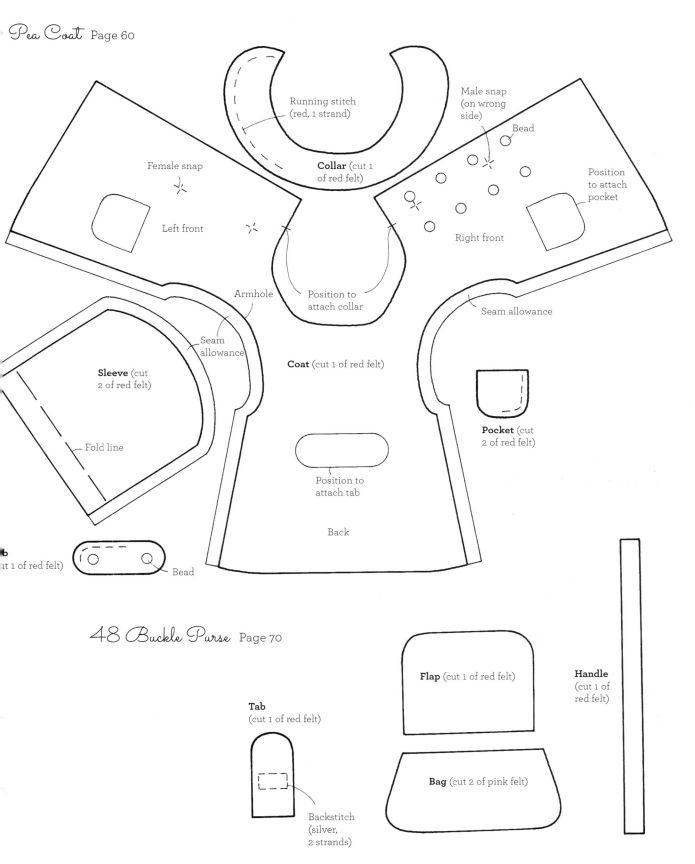

Pea Coat Page 60

Running stitch
(red, 1 strand)

Collar (cut 1
of red felt)

Male snap
(on wrong
side)

Bead

Female snap

Position
to attach
pocket

Left front

Right front

Armhole

Position to
attach collar

Seam
allowance

Seam allowance

Sleeve (cut
2 of red felt)

Coat (cut 1 of red felt)

Pocket (cut
2 of red felt)

Fold line

Position to
attach tab

Back

b
ut 1 of red felt)

Bead

48 Buckle Purse Page 70

Flap (cut 1 of red felt)

Handle
(cut 1 of
red felt)

Tab
(cut 1 of red felt)

Bag (cut 2 of pink felt)

Backstitch
(silver,
2 strands)

53 Rosette Collar Page 66

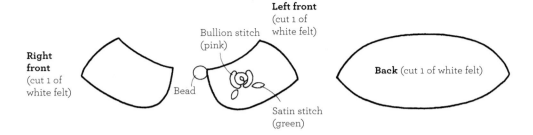

Right front
(cut 1 of white felt)

Left front
(cut 1 of white felt)

Bullion stitch
(pink)

Bead

Satin stitch
(green)

Back (cut 1 of white felt)

35 Hooded Cape Page 59

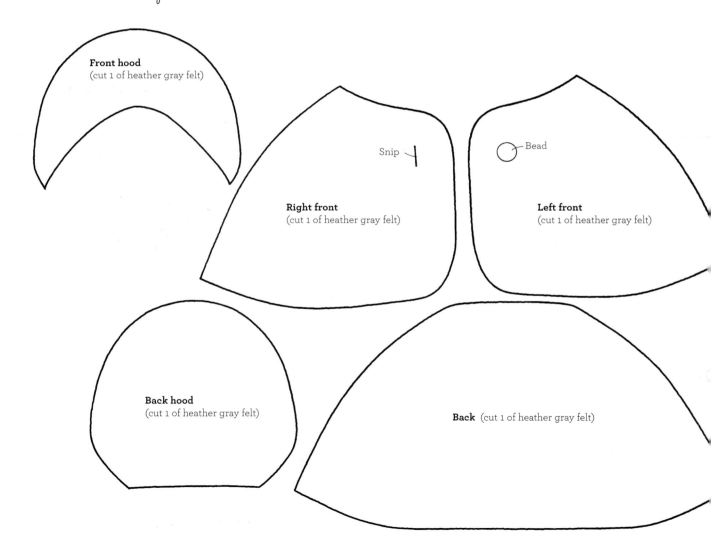

Front hood
(cut 1 of heather gray felt)

Snip

Bead

Right front
(cut 1 of heather gray felt)

Left front
(cut 1 of heather gray felt)

Back hood
(cut 1 of heather gray felt)

Back (cut 1 of heather gray felt)

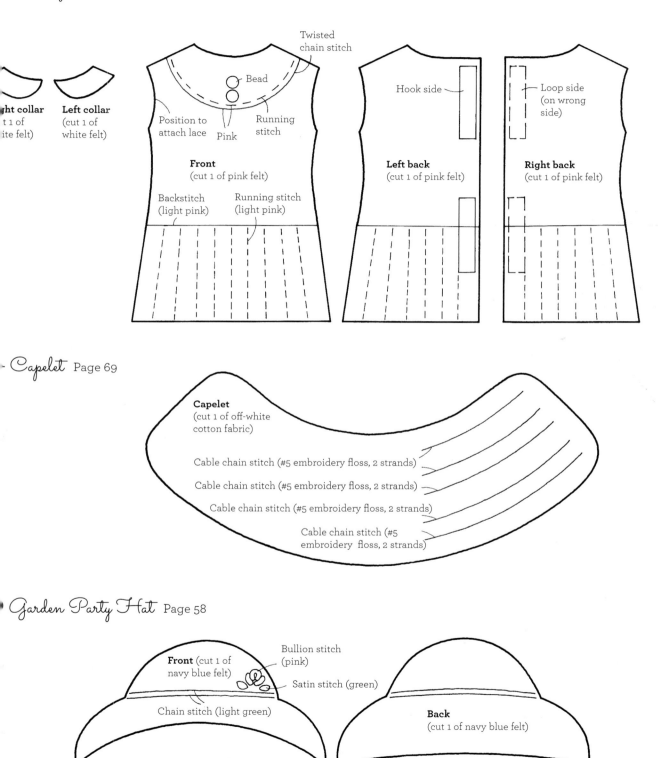

Frilly Dress Page 65

Right collar
(cut 1 of white felt)

Left collar
(cut 1 of white felt)

Twisted chain stitch

Bead

Position to attach lace

Pink

Running stitch

Front
(cut 1 of pink felt)

Backstitch (light pink)

Running stitch (light pink)

Hook side

Left back
(cut 1 of pink felt)

Loop side (on wrong side)

Right back
(cut 1 of pink felt)

Capelet Page 69

Capelet
(cut 1 of off-white cotton fabric)

Cable chain stitch (#5 embroidery floss, 2 strands)

Cable chain stitch (#5 embroidery floss, 2 strands)

Cable chain stitch (#5 embroidery floss, 2 strands)

Cable chain stitch (#5 embroidery floss, 2 strands)

Garden Party Hat Page 58

Front (cut 1 of navy blue felt)

Bullion stitch (pink)

Satin stitch (green)

Chain stitch (light green)

Back
(cut 1 of navy blue felt)

Kate and Lisa
Page 78

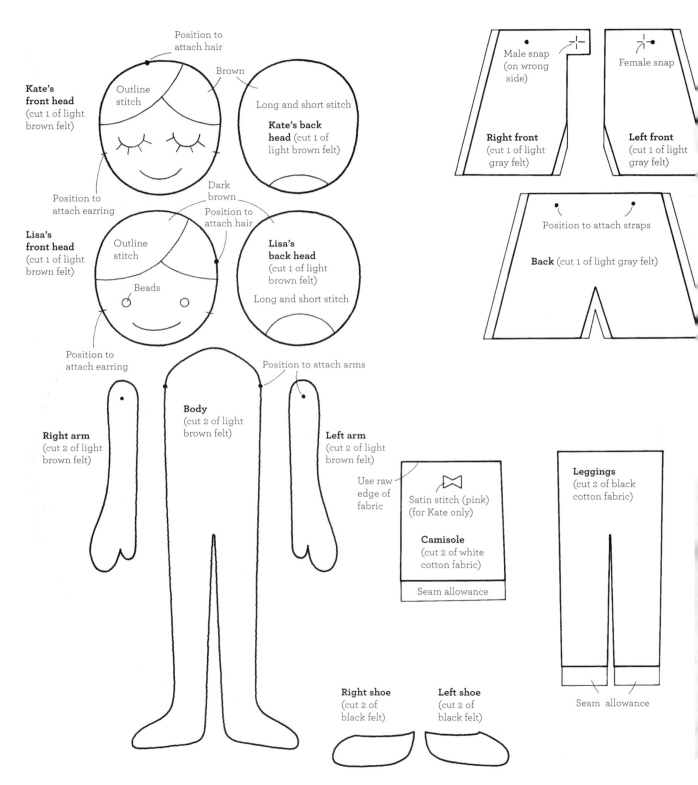

Position to attach hair

Brown

Kate's front head (cut 1 of light brown felt)

Outline stitch

Long and short stitch

Kate's back head (cut 1 of light brown felt)

Position to attach earring

Dark brown

Position to attach hair

Lisa's front head (cut 1 of light brown felt)

Outline stitch

Lisa's back head (cut 1 of light brown felt)

Long and short stitch

Beads

Position to attach earring

Position to attach arms

Body (cut 2 of light brown felt)

Right arm (cut 2 of light brown felt)

Left arm (cut 2 of light brown felt)

Male snap (on wrong side)

Female snap

Right front (cut 1 of light gray felt)

Left front (cut 1 of light gray felt)

Position to attach straps

Back (cut 1 of light gray felt)

Use raw edge of fabric

Satin stitch (pink) (for Kate only)

Camisole (cut 2 of white cotton fabric)

Seam allowance

Leggings (cut 2 of black cotton fabric)

Seam allowance

Right shoe (cut 2 of black felt)

Left shoe (cut 2 of black felt)

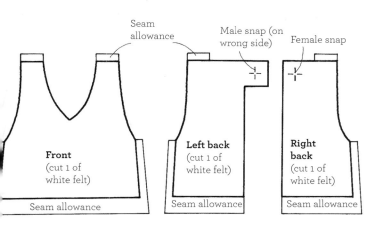

Ballet Dress Page 82

Seam allowance

Male snap (on wrong side)

Female snap

Front
(cut 1 of white felt)

Seam allowance

Left back
(cut 1 of white felt)

Seam allowance

Right back
(cut 1 of white felt)

Seam allowance

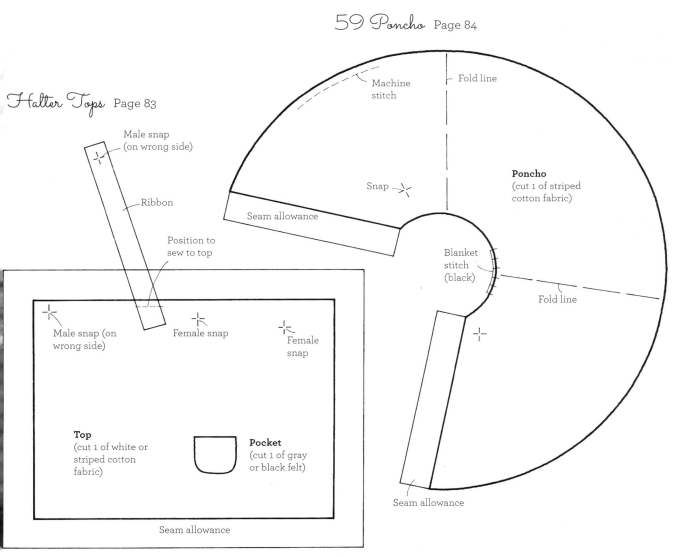

59 Poncho Page 84

Halter Tops Page 83

Machine stitch

Fold line

Male snap (on wrong side)

Ribbon

Snap

Poncho
(cut 1 of striped cotton fabric)

Position to sew to top

Seam allowance

Blanket stitch (black)

Fold line

Male snap (on wrong side)

Female snap

Female snap

Top
(cut 1 of white or striped cotton fabric)

Pocket
(cut 1 of gray or black felt)

Seam allowance

Seam allowance

61 Romper Page 86

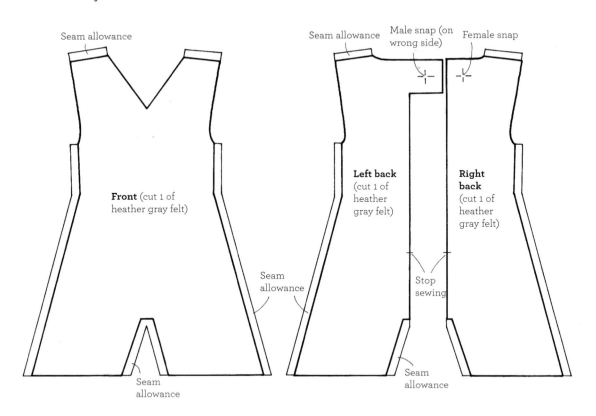

Seam allowance

Front (cut 1 of heather gray felt)

Seam allowance

Seam allowance

Seam allowance

Male snap (on wrong side)

Female snap

Left back (cut 1 of heather gray felt)

Right back (cut 1 of heather gray felt)

Stop sewing

Seam allowance

60 Tulle Tank Page 85

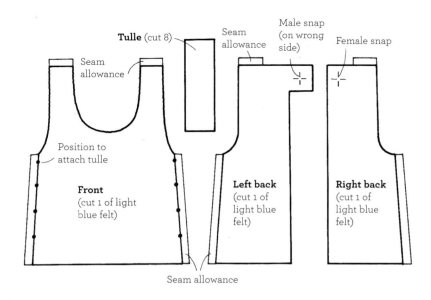

Tulle (cut 8)

Seam allowance

Seam allowance

Position to attach tulle

Front (cut 1 of light blue felt)

Male snap (on wrong side)

Female snap

Left back (cut 1 of light blue felt)

Right back (cut 1 of light blue felt)

Seam allowance

64 Chain Strap Purse, 65 Classic Purse, and 66 Mini Pochettes
Page 87

Back (cut 1 of felt)

Front (cut 1 of felt)